Advance Praise for *Radical Welcome*

"This is not a 'feel good' book. It is not about how we should all be nice to strangers at coffee hour. This is a book about the very hard challenges that face any of us when we decide to step outside of our isolation for the sake of the gospel. . . . [T]his book is that rare combination of deep spirituality and pragmatism. . . . The call to take on the challenges of 'radical welcome' is for the growth of the community, not only in numbers, but in spirit, imagination, and strength. This is a book about the future envisioned by the gospel, a future that extends the love of Christ in all directions."

—From the foreword by Stephen Charleston,
author of *The Four Vision Quests of Jesus*
and former Bishop of Alaska and Dean of Episcopal Divinity School

"The beautiful thing about re-revisiting *Radical Welcome* fifteen years on is discovering that it has a timelessness and relevance that we critically need today. . . . The vision of who we can be, truly reflecting the image of God, is stunningly beautiful and more than worth the effort."

—The Rt. Rev. Jennifer Baskerville-Burrows
Bishop of the Episcopal Diocese of Indianapolis

"When I read *Radical Welcome* fifteen years ago, I knew that it was deeply thoughtful and theologically grounded. I didn't—couldn't have—known that it was also futuristic, even prophetic. Today, a much wider audience is seeking to embrace diversity in ways that are authentically faithful rather than simply socially tasteful, 'woke,' and de rigueur. I am grateful to have this resource to read again, with its new essays and updates, and to commend it to those who are becoming aware of the intentionality building a truly welcoming community requires."

—Sarah B. Drummond
Founding Dean, Andover Newton Seminary at Yale Divinity School

Radical
Welcome

STEPHANIE SPELLERS

Radical
Welcome

Embracing God, The Other and
the Spirit of Transformation

Morehouse Publishing
NEW YORK

Morehouse Publishing, 19 East 34th Street, New York, NY 10016

Morehouse Publishing is an imprint of Church Publishing Incorporated.

Cover photo by JannHuizenga
Cover design by Jennifer Kopec, 2Pug Design
Typeset by Rose Design

Library of Congress Cataloging-in-Publication Data

Names: Spellers, Stephanie, author.
Title: Radical welcome : embracing God, the other, and the spirit of transformation / Stephanie Spellers.
Description: 15th anniversary edition. | New York, NY : Morehouse Publishing, [2021] | Includes bibliographical references.
Identifiers: LCCN 2021040188 (print) | LCCN 2021040189 (ebook) | ISBN 9781640654686 (paperback) | ISBN 9781640654693 (ebook)
Subjects: LCSH: Non-church-affiliated people. | Church work with ex-church members. | Evangelistic work. | Church growth. | Church development, New.
Classification: LCC BV4921.2 .S68 2021 (print) | LCC BV4921.2 (ebook) | DDC 253--dc23
LC record available at https://lccn.loc.gov/2021040188
LC ebook record available at https://lccn.loc.gov/2021040189

For my mother, Phyllis Spellers,
my biggest cheerleader and inspiration,
who says she always knew I'd write a book someday.

And for my entire family in Frankfort, Kentucky,
who taught me how to swing open the doors
and invite the whole community to the table.

Contents

Foreword

One of my fondest memories is about a parish I served many years ago. It was in the housing projects. It met upstairs over a local café. I described it as a "half-way house" because so many of our folks had either left the church and were now half-way back in, or they were half-way out of the church and were just giving it one more try before they gave up. It was a great community. A porous, challenging, engaged community. A place full of unique and extraordinary people.

After reading Stephanie Speller's book, *Radical Welcome: Embracing God, The Other and the Spirit of Transformation*, I realize that more than a half-way house, my parish was actually a place of radical welcome. We were an experiment in acceptance. I never would have made that connection in quite the same way without the language of radical welcome.

"We will consider the rationale for radical welcome," Stephanie writes in the opening to her remarkable book, "and then explore the resources people engaged in the movement toward radical welcome told me they found the most essential—and the hardest to find."

And that's just what she does. She gives us a framework and she gives us practical tools. In a step-by-step journey of discovery into what radical welcome is and how it can work, Stephanie offers us a blueprint for planned growth, change, and mission. She shows us that there is a great, untapped source of strength for every congregation. It is the presence of The Other within the pastoral neighborhood: that group of persons who stand just beyond the social/cultural threshold of the congregation. Engaging them honestly will not only expand the horizons of the congregation but revitalize it in ways that could never be realized otherwise. In simple language, radical welcome shows us how we need one another, and even more importantly, how we translate that potential into the blessings of a church renewed.

She is also honest about how hard the job will be. This is not a "feel good" book. It is not about how we should all be nice to strangers at coffee hour. This is a book about the very hard challenges that face any of us when we decide to step outside of our isolation for the sake of the gospel.

To make a commitment to explore the depth of what radical welcome means, we are asked to confront how we all "participate in systems of inclusion and exclusion." We are asked to deal with the fact that in practicing radical welcome "there is no such place as a neutral space."

In short, Stephanie is calling us to a much more mature and nuanced understanding of what it means for any congregation to truly open its doors to community. It is not a matter of just accepting difference. It is a matter of creating something new. Her book is a resource because it tells the story of how real congregations achieved remarkable results in allowing the chemistry of human cultures to mix more freely to produce a people of faith. This is not theory but practice. It is an articulation of the basic steps that any community of faith would need to take to experience transformation and renewal.

Consequently, this book is that rare combination of deep spirituality and pragmatism. Much like the Holy Scriptures on which it is firmly grounded, Stephanie's vision of radical welcome talks about new life for the people of God. The call to take on the challenges of "radical welcome" is for the growth of the community, not only in numbers, but in spirit, imagination and strength. This is a book about the future envisioned by the gospel, a future that extends the love of Christ in all directions.

I believe that at its heart, radical welcome is about the new definition of evangelism for the twenty-first century. In the past, we have consigned evangelism to the simple exercise of duplication: creating more communities in our own image. In response to the cultural changes of the Civil Rights Movement and up to the present day, we have often spoken of evangelism as though it were sensitivity training for cross-cultural special events. What Stephanie is suggesting is something very different.

Radical welcome is not the welcome wagon. Her direction moves us through the mono-cultural dead end of traditional images of evangelism and beyond the boundaries of polite cultural interaction. It takes us directly to the heart of the nature of evangelism: the transformation of human life from the isolated to the integrated.

Radical welcome is a process. It is a process by which isolated parts of a whole community are brought together in creative and compassionate ways to generate a more integrated, balanced, and dynamic mixture. Not a melting pot or a stew of differences, but a community that works well, prays well, and plans well together. These communities are grounded in some of the most basic values we share as God's people. Radical welcome describes how communities stay hospitable, connected, centered, open to conversion, and intentional. These are fundamental qualities for any meaningful congregational experience. They are, in short, what pastors are looking for. What radical welcome offers are methods and practices that bring the gospel alive in communities that work for everyone, not just for the few.

"Radical welcome is a fundamental spiritual practice," Stephanie writes, and that is precisely what she offers here. This is a book about renewal. About growth. About intelligent change. I believe that any person who cares for authentic ministry in open and affirming ways will find a home in radical welcome. This is a resource many of us have been waiting for. It is a message whose time has come.

I hope you enjoy reading *Radical Welcome* as much as I did. I hope even more that you will share it with others. And finally, I hope most of all that you will put its lessons to work as you extend God's radical welcome to every person without whom your community would not be complete.

The Rt. Rev. Steven Charleston
Episcopal Divinity School
Cambridge, Massachusetts
August 2006

Introduction to the 15th Anniversary Edition

[Jesus] said . . . "Therefore every scribe who has been trained
for the kingdom of heaven is like the master of a household who
brings out of his treasure what is new and what is old."

MATTHEW 13:52

It has been fifteen years since the publication of *Radical Welcome: Embracing God, The Other and the Spirit of Transformation*. In those years, so much has changed. So much more has not.

Back in 2006, my church was in a fight for its life. Following the consecration of the Rt. Rev. Gene Robinson as bishop of the Diocese of New Hampshire in 2003, the Episcopal Church was torn asunder and ostracized from much of the global Anglican Communion. Though we had been on record since 1976 supporting the pastoral care and welcome of same-gender loving people, and though we had (also in 1976) consented to women's ordination to the priesthood and even episcopacy, still members and leaders struggled, legislated, and prayed over the nature of inclusion. How would the church incorporate and lift homosexual people's voices, gifts, wisdom, and power? Would the church welcome voices, gifts, wisdom, and power from the margins at all?

At that time, I sensed the limits of inclusion and welcome. As an African American, working-class-identified, young adult woman in a church built around White, male, upper-class culture and norms, I was more than familiar with the church's push-pull around inclusion. It says it wants certain groups, says it supports and values us, only to undermine, marginalize, or silence us if we do or say that which does not advance the dominant culture and agenda. In other words, mainline churches love young people who play Bach cantatas and Latinx people who have mastered Robert's Rules, while they tend to hold at bay Afro-Caribbean people who are not "high church" and LGBTQ people who are a bit too "queer." The institution wants diversity for decoration, to assuage guilt, and, yes, to address the sin of oppression—but generally on its own terms. It knows how to dominate and assimilate. Mutuality is a dream.

Radical Welcome felt like a cry in the wilderness. As I read today the names of the people and places I visited and chronicled in these pages, I am struck by the spirit of rebellion, deep faithfulness, hovering loneliness, and boundless hope. We had heard about the dream of God. We had pledged as Episcopalians to seek and serve Christ in all persons, to love our neighbors as ourselves, to strive for justice and peace among all people, and to respect the dignity of every human being—and now we wanted to be in a church that lived out those radical claims. We were eager to offer our hearts and gifts to serve God's mission, but we also dreamt of bringing our whole hearts and truly diverse array of gifts, cultures, voices, and power into the mix. We knew it would change us, change our sibling Christians in the dominant culture, and change the church as a whole . . . and we trusted that mutual transformation was an essential element of the Spirit's wild and wonderful plan for creation.

That's what inspired me to invite my own Episcopal church and others like it to push beyond mere inclusion and to take on radical welcome. The definition below—which I refined after a few more years of teaching and journeying—continues to resonate and challenge:

> Radical welcome is first and foremost a spiritual practice. It combines the Christian ministry of welcome and hospitality with a faithful commitment to doing the theological, spiritual, and systemic work to eliminate historic, systemic barriers that deny the genuine embrace of groups often oppressed and marginalized in mainline churches.
>
> As you practice radical welcome, you join Jesus in stretching your arms and embracing The Other. You share the gifts of your tradition and culture, even as you allow your heart and your congregation's life—its ministries, its identity, its worship, its relationships, its leadership—to be transformed by The Other's presence, gifts, and power among you.

As you read those words and the ones that follow, I hope you hear the call as truly radical. Lots of churches use the phrase "radical welcome" only to engage in almost no power analysis and to take very few steps beyond inclusion, acquisition, and diversity. Sometimes I wish the word "welcome" didn't sound so warm and nice, and thus so easy to domesticate. People can focus on the "Christian ministry of welcome and hospitality" part and glide right past "the theological, spiritual, and systemic work to eliminate historic, systemic barriers that deny the genuine embrace of groups often oppressed and marginalized in mainline churches."

Please don't let that happen. Especially now—while the atmosphere swirls with #metoo, racial reckoning, populism, and an ever-broadening spectrum of gender and sexuality—this is a moment to dig more deeply into the hard work of dismantling the historic and systemic barriers that have made it nearly impossible for mainline churches to fully embrace (not just include but embrace and be changed by) the oppressed. We have clearer language, better tools, and more people than ever ready to invest in transformation and not merely cosmetic change.

Please don't just read and assume we've already mastered this work. Instead, ask God to reveal how you might (re)commit to the spiritual practice of radical welcome. Wonder anew what margins and edges Jesus is leading you toward, whether outside or inside. For instance, many Episcopalians pat the church on the back for fully welcoming lesbian, gay, bisexual, transgender, queer, and questioning peoples. Meanwhile, LGBTQ peoples—especially those who lack the privilege of Whiteness or class—are waving their arms and yelling, "Not so fast! You may feel heard and powerful, but we do not."

Their voices and witness remind me that the work of inclusion and welcome is not finished. Every person and every institution has an Other on the edge. The edge for you may be a cultural group or behavior that still grates and feels like it's just not appropriate or holy. The edge may be something in yourself that you've tried to shove down and replace with behaviors that the dominant culture affirms and rewards. Where and who is the Spirit calling you to embrace?

As I say this, I know that even radical welcome is not the end of the story. "Welcome" still conjures the dynamics of inside and outside, with different groups on different sides of the threshold. To speak of "welcome" is still to center the one in power, the one who gets to decide who comes in and who does not. Yes, we are both changed, but someone owns the house and the table. Someone decides if The Other is "welcome" or not.

In an age when the church has been decentered (or what I call "cracked open") as a building and as an institution, the point is not only to make room inside the church but to discover and dwell with Jesus and make a life with him beyond what we've understood as church. By this, I don't just mean leaving the building, though for a time the COVID-19 pandemic forced us to do just that. I actually mean a fundamental reimagining of church as the community of Jesus' followers who align ourselves with his self-giving ways and his love for the crucified, the forgotten, the ultimate Other.

I've engaged these ideas much more fully in a recent book called, *The Church Cracked Open: Disruption, Decline, and New Hope for Beloved Community*. As I revisit *Radical Welcome*, I can't help but see the two books as companions or two sides of the same coin. *Radical Welcome* focuses more on changing the life and practice of a congregation, ministry, or institution. *The Church Cracked Open* decenters the church and focuses more on the spiritual yet practical journey away from empire and White supremacy toward discipleship and beloved community.

We still need radical welcome in order to fully embrace the voices, gifts, cultures, and power of nondominant communities. We need it in order fundamentally to transform the ministry, leadership, and worship of our churches, so they become embodiments of the gospel of Jesus Christ. And we need more.

What's New?

Since 2006, so much has changed—and so much has not—in our churches and in the world. It makes sense that this new edition should include the core material as well as some new reflections. What will you find in this expanded edition?

1. The essence of the book remains, largely untouched:

   - The opening section defines "radical welcome" and introduces the eight churches at the core of the Radical Welcome Project.
   - The chapters in Part I explore the theology and practical spirituality of radical welcome—including God's heart for welcome, community, and transformation—and God's invitation to radically surrender to the Spirit and to live without fear.
   - Part II offers a picture of radical welcome—with critical material that differentiates between "Inviting," "Inclusion," and "Radical Welcome," and points the way toward becoming a multicultural, anti-racist organization (many thanks to Crossroads for permission to use their popular continuum)—along with a framework for identifying the "Radical Welcome Signs" in these five elements of a congregation's life:

     — Mission and vision
     — Identity
     — Ministries and relationships
     — Leadership and feedback systems
     — Worship

   - The rubber hits the road in Part III. This is the longest section, with detailed practical support for not just talking but making real change. For each element of congregational life, you'll find questions for assessing "Where Are We Now?" and then charting a course for "Where Is God Inviting Us to Go?" This section also acknowledges major strategic concerns for practicing radical welcome, including how to examine your congregation's deeper narratives, history, and identity; and how to reckon pastorally and practically with fear—and yes, everyone has it to some degree, whether that's fear of The Other or fear of change.

- The section ends with a fully updated chapter on "Where Do We Go from Here . . . Now?" which lays out possible next steps and the essential practices of a radically welcoming community.

2. Other notes on the original edition:

- I struggled over whether to update the biographical details of the people whose voices and wisdom appear throughout this book. In the end, I opted to leave them as written, because it's important to keep their reflections rooted in the actual context where they were offered.

- I confess that I was prepared to rewrite much of Part III on practice, until I found myself genuinely surprised by how much continues to apply. I hope you will agree.

- The resources sprinkled throughout the book hold up surprisingly well. That said, I've supplemented the online resources wth newer material and updated web addresses wherever necessary.

- Where you see "congregation," feel free to insert "ministry" or "institution" or "community." Though my research focused on congregations, I've since worked with plenty of independent schools, diocesan teams, and other groups that found the theology, principles, and practice of radical welcome speaks to their dreams and challenges quite well.

3. Along with the reimagined chapter on next steps, you'll be blessed by four new essays from noted colleagues reflecting on the practice of radical welcome and how it intersects with their ministries and their understanding of church.

- Mark Bozzuti-Jones, priest and director of Spiritual Formation for Trinity Church–Wall Street in New York City, offers a poetic take on radical welcome.

- Bishop Jennifer Baskerville-Burrows notes how radical welcome has been a constant companion, from her years as a priest in a multicultural, multi-generational parish in upstate New York, to her service as a canon in the Diocese of Chicago and now in her role as the bishop of Indianapolis.

- W. Mark Richardson, president and dean of the Church Divinity School of the Pacific in Berkeley, California, examines radical welcome, mutuality, and community organizing, and their impact on his own ministry, his institution, and theological formation.
- In 2006, Bishop Michael Curry was a beloved teacher and preacher across the land and the first Black person to lead a southern diocese in the Episcopal Church. Today he is the church's first black presiding bishop and is known around the world. He reflects on the dream of God, radical welcome, and making our ideas and arms stretch as wide as the embrace of our God.
- Finally, I have written a new concluding chapter about the challenges of radical welcome and some compelling lessons from nearly twenty years engaging churches and leaders in this conversation.

4. And because *Radical Welcome* was never meant to be just a book, the robust web resource titled "Bread for the Journey" features original and updated small group studies, handouts and exercises, sermons, a bible study, annotated bibliography, and more. Find these goods at www.stephaniespellers.com/radical-welcome.

Before we embark, I must say "thank you" to the thousands of people who have walked the road toward radical welcome with me over these many years. You have taught and blessed me and one another, and I feel you at my side now as I revisit and revise. With your help, I hope to be like those kingdom scribes Jesus noticed in Matthew 13, the ones who gather some that is old and some that is new, weaving and discerning and ultimately presenting the final offering with the prayer that it may serve the dream of God. May it be so, in the power of the Spirit.

Stephanie Spellers
Harlem, New York
Pentecost 2021

Introduction to Radical Welcome

The Radical
Welcome Journey

Come we that love the Lord,
and let our joys be known;

Join in a song of sweet accord,
join in a song of sweet accord,

And thus surround the throne,
and thus surround the throne.

We're marching to Zion,
beautiful, beautiful Zion,

We're marching upward to Zion,
the beautiful city of God.

"Marching to Zion"

A Tale of Two Welcomes

I will never forget that winter's day, sitting in the Cathedral of St. John the Divine, a grand Gothic edifice on New York's Upper West Side. Though I had worshiped on the fringe of the congregation while living, working and writing in the city, this time I had come simply to celebrate a friend's ordination.

Seated at the back of the church, distant from the action at the front of the chancel, I was slowly, inexorably tuning out. And then, with a sharp visceral tug, I tuned back in.

"Lord, I will lift mine eyes to the hills, knowing my help, it comes from you . . ."

Was I hearing right?

"Your peace you give me in times of the storm. You are the source of my strength . . ."

Could it be?

"You are the strength of my life."

Oh my God, that was it!

"I lift my hands in total praise."

Like a giddy child, I turned to my friends on either side, whispering, "Do you hear it? Do you hear it?" They nodded, but they really didn't have a clue.

On the surface, we all heard a magnificent quartet from a local black church singing Richard Smallwood's "Total Praise." What I and perhaps a few others could hear was sweet memory. My mama used to play "Total Praise" on those random Sundays when she would pack me and my brother into the Oldsmobile Omega and cart us to the African Methodist Episcopal Zion Church in Knoxville, Tennessee. Later, I sang in some school-based gospel choirs and cobbled together my own gospel music collection. Even later, once I landed in the Episcopal Church, I played the songs religiously while I dressed for church, my private time to "get my praise on." But hearing this music—a pop gospel hymn sung by soaring, expressive black voices—in an immense, dignified, European-American identified space? The tears poured, my hands waved, I lifted my voice, and deep inside I heaved a huge sigh of relief and gratitude for the welcome.

Years after my official reception into the Episcopal Church, a part of me that I didn't even know was sitting outside finally opened the door and came in.

Rewind a decade. It was the early 1990s, toward the end of my first year of divinity school, and I had just arrived at an Episcopal guest house in a major U.S. city. Mind you, I wasn't Episcopalian. I wasn't technically even Christian yet (I liked to study it and sing about it, but that was my limit). Still, coming to the door of the lovely building was like coming to a God-filled oasis for this country girl.

The host appeared at the door and asked how much I would be paying before I could step inside. I hopefully mentioned the sliding scale their materials advertised. The host offered to take $20 off the price *if* I didn't eat meals with the community. It was still pricey, especially if I had to arrange my own food. The host smiled, suggested I try the nearby youth hostel, and shut the door, leaving a single, petite, young, black woman with limited financial resources and no place to go on the doorstep.

I walked away wondering what kind of religious community, and what kind of church, these Episcopalians had created. Whatever it was, I was sure it was not very Christian. And needless to say, it was radically *un*welcoming.

I kept my distance from Episcopalians after that encounter. But the God of surprises had a shock tucked away for me. A few years later, I was baptized at a remarkable multicultural Lutheran parish in Boston, and even considered ordination in the Lutheran fold. But something still hadn't clicked. Then I discovered St. Peter's Episcopal Church in Cambridge, Massachusetts, a vibrant city congregation filled with people of color and whites; heterosexuals, lesbians, gay men, bisexual people, and transgender people; young adults, some youth, middle-aged people, and seniors; poor and middle-class people rubbing shoulders with the Cambridge elite.

Not only did this mixed-up community feel like home, but the Anglican theology I was voraciously consuming resonated with my own latent sense of what a lived faith ought to be. I needed a comprehensive theology that tolerates ambiguity and acknowledges that no single perspective could ever capture the mind of God. I needed to join a body of people who maintain a reverence for tradition and Scripture alongside a deep respect for reason and context. I wanted the awe, the mess, the beauty, the poetry. I craved the emphasis on justice rooted in an incarnational, resurrection-focused faith. I had found it.

But that experience of welcome did not erase the memory of a door shut in my face years before. Yes, I have witnessed the enthusiastic response when a mostly white congregation sings that rare gospel tune, and I have quietly rejoiced when others remarked, "Why don't we sing this music more often? It's like something in me wakes up and starts to praise God again." But far more often, I have suffered the snide comments about evangelical and gospel music that is not "theologically sophisticated" enough for our churches. I have heard or read leaders of supposedly welcoming churches saying they don't want to "dumb down" their sermons or programs, or to water down their identity, in order to accommodate different races, classes and generations. As a thirtysomething person of color raised in the working-class South, I've had to continually set aside the hope of hearing and seeing the voices, images, stories, and values of my home culture incorporated regularly in any but the most intentionally welcoming mainline churches.

And I am not alone.

We are already here: the strangers, the outcasts, the poor, people of color, gay and lesbian people, young adults, and so many more. We resonate with our church's theology and traditions. We love our congregations and pray and labor for their health, growth and ministry.

That doesn't mean we feel welcome.

This conflicted experience has led me to wonder what it would take to reverse the effect of years, if not generations, of alienation, marginalization and outright rejection. Is it even possible to transform mainline churches into the multicultural, multigenerational, inclusive body of Christ so many of us yearn to become?

That's where radical welcome comes in.

Radical welcome[1] is the spiritual practice of embracing and being changed by the gifts, presence, voices, and power of The Other: the people systemically cast out of or marginalized within a church, a denomination and/or society. Your church may be predominantly white or Latino, wealthy or working-class, gay or straight, middle-aged or fairly young. Regardless of your demographic profile, you still have a margin, a disempowered Other who is in your midst or just outside your door. In fact, you may be The Other. Radical welcome is concerned with the transformation and opening of individual hearts, congregations and systems so that The Other might find in your community a warm place and a mutual embrace *and* so that you are finally free to embrace and be transformed by authentic relationship with the margins.

The Radical Welcome Project

My survival in the church has depended on finding communities devoted to extending radical welcome. I first saw them in relative abundance on a study tour in the Episcopal Diocese of Los Angeles. But what if you couldn't get to L.A. or some other oasis? Where were their stories, and how could others learn from their experiences?

I dusted off my reporter's cap that summer and set out to examine eight churches moving toward fully embracing The Other in what I called "The Radical Welcome Project." Those congregations were Grace Church in Lawrence, Massachusetts; St. Philip's and St. Mary's, both in Harlem, New York; St. Bartholomew's in Atlanta, Georgia; St. Paul's in Duluth, Minnesota; All Saints in Pasadena, California; Holy Faith in Inglewood, California; and Church of the Apostles in Seattle, Washington. I consciously chose to focus

---

1. The term *radical welcome* has cropped up independently in various communities over the past decade or so. I coined the phrase for my own use after colleagues demanded a concise descriptor for the broadly inclusive churches I was beginning to study. My initial project—spending four months conducting intensive, on-site research with eight congregations nationwide—was called the Radical Welcome Project.

Later, I discovered leaders at St. Bartholomew's Episcopal Church in New York City use the same term to characterize their ministry to all God's people, especially seekers and lesbian, gay, bisexual, and transgendered (LGBT) people. Other groups in the "welcoming congregations" movement—which seeks total inclusion for LGBT people—have expanded the idea of welcoming so that it encompasses an even broader community of outcasts. They landed at radical welcome by a natural evolutionary process.

on the unique hopes and challenges of a selection of Episcopal churches, trusting that ultimately their struggles and insights would also prove useful across denominational contexts.

The sample covers small, medium and corporate-sized churches and draws from the coasts, the heartland and the South, as well as the suburbs, large cities and smaller communities. Most importantly, I wanted to study churches that ran the gamut in terms of community composition and who and how they were welcoming. In particular, I opted to focus on how each dealt with embracing across lines of race and ethnicity, generation, sexual orientation, and class privilege. Some wrestled with one issue, most with a combination. No one had the same margins or the same center, so the lessons are truly broad in their application.

In each congregation, I conducted in-depth research over the course of two weeks, including advance interviews and parish-written histories and other introductory materials, followed by at least ten days spent attending services, programs, meetings, and informal conversations, and concluding with follow-up contacts as necessary. My study of these congregations was less a precise social scientific study than an exploration and exercise in deep listening. Along the way, we talked about where they started, where they are now, and what steps they took along the way. We discussed how they welcome people from the margins, who The Other is for them, why they've taken up this Christian practice, what has proved most challenging on the road to radical welcome, and what barriers remain. They told me of their successes, their hopes and their failures, admitting that they were far from perfect, still met plenty of resistance, and sometimes fell off the path. And so, while these may not be the most radically welcoming churches anywhere, I came to value them for their sheer humanity and humility: they fall short and they keep trying, the momentum has waxed and waned, and that's part of the wisdom they can pass along to the rest of us.

There are lots of radically welcoming Episcopal congregations nationwide and plenty more outside the Episcopal fold, and I've taken care to talk with representatives from a number of these communities. Over the past several years, I've interviewed more than 200 lay leaders, clergy, professors, seminarians, liturgists, change leaders at the local and national levels, and other observers, all of whom shared wise reflections on change, welcome, fear, church history, theology, Scripture, and more.

In the pages that follow, you will hear these voices in a lively conversation with the writings of the faithful, from the Hebrew Scriptures and New Testament through centuries of Christian theology leading to contemporary teachers throughout the Christian tradition and beyond our fold. Finally, I've incorporated insights drawn from my experience in faith-based community organizing and from consulting and sharing this material in communities considering or already committed to transformational growth. All this wisdom is compiled here and offered as bread for your journey.

Your Radical Welcome Journey

Has God whispered in your ear or tugged your sleeve, urging you to step off the curb and onto this road? You're in the right place now, especially if . . .

- your neighborhood has changed—maybe there are more people of color or young people or poor people or lesbian, gay, bisexual, and transgendered people—and while you want to do the "right" thing, you have no idea where to start.
- you are one of The Others within a congregation, and you hope to spark or nurture your community's commitment to transformation and find nourishment so that you can persevere.
- your church and area are homogeneous (or seem to be), but you still feel called to radical welcome as a spiritual practice—one that trains and stretches your heart to receive more of God, to surrender to the surprising, transforming movement of the Holy Spirit—and you want to find those opportunities to say "yes" to God and to The Other.
- you want to learn the basic language of radical welcome and wrap your mind and tongue around a term that's getting more airplay everyday.
- you hope to move deeper, to get grounded in the biblical and theological issues surrounding and supporting radical welcome and perhaps to share those foundational insights with others in your congregation and community.
- you know you want to see your church become radically welcoming, but you could use some concrete examples and inspiring images of other congregations that have walked this road for a while, to see for yourself how it works.
- you're ready to cast your own radically welcoming vision, to imagine in Technicolor what would happen at your church if you embraced fresh words, voices, songs, and faces, all standing alongside the wise, revered traditions and voices that have grounded your church's identity so far;
- or you've already begun the journey toward radical change, but now you need to reckon with your history, fear (your own and others'), complacency, or a host of other challenges along the way.

This book is far more than a how-to guide for quickly achieving those goals. Rather, in the chapters that follow, I invite you to be part of a journey.

Along the way, we will consider the biblical and theological foundations for radical welcome, explore vivid pictures of the dream come to life in several communities, and the resources people engaged in the work told me they found most essential—and hardest to find. You can take it to the next level using the book's online companion—"Bread for the Journey"—which includes exercises, Bible studies, charts, strategic planning tips, and a workshop for congregations.

As you read, examine and move forward, I hope you will be patient with yourself and your community. Please stay rooted in hope, rather than paralyzing guilt or finger-pointing (at yourself or others). Try to be honest about your story, your privilege and your fears. Don't be afraid to keep asking, "What new thing is God calling me to be and to do?" and "What support, education, training and practices would help me to follow through on what I now imagine for myself and my congregation?" The road into new life is a long one, and this leg of the journey is designed to stretch your imagination, fuel your passion and guide you closer to God's radically welcoming dream for us all.

Defining Radical Welcome

It's time to bring a different set of questions.
Not just how do we get more people, but how do we
share power, how do you create a culture that is flexible
and fluid enough to be open, constantly evaluating and
reorganizing based on the reality around you?

THE REVEREND ALTAGRACIA PEREZ,
HOLY FAITH EPISCOPAL CHURCH, INGLEWOOD, CALIFORNIA

Just what is radical welcome? Most people hear the term and think it's about having a warm, dependable welcome at the door of the church and a really good cup of coffee and snacks in the church hall. They assume it's the province of the Hospitality and Greeters Committee or maybe, just maybe, the Outreach and Justice group.

Those are wonderful goals. But that's not where radical welcome is aiming. Radical welcome is a fundamental spiritual practice, one that combines the universal Christian ministry of welcome and hospitality with a clear awareness of power[1] and patterns of inclusion and exclusion.

Just look at the words. Radical. Welcome. Both terms are rich with meaning. *Welcome* says come in, sit down, stay a while; we are honored

---

1. I appreciate Sheryl Kujawa-Holbrook's definition of power in her work on multiracial communities; she describes it as "the capacity to have control, authority or influence over others. [In particular] social power refers to the capacity of the dominant culture to have control, authority and influence over" oppressed peoples. She concludes, "social power plus prejudice equals oppression." See *A House of Prayer for All Peoples: Building Multiracial Community* (Bethesda, MD: Alban Institute, 2004), 15.

to have you. It also says the door is open, a bit like, "You're welcome to whatever is in the fridge." And it indicates an openness of spirit, that what we do is a pleasure. When someone thanks you for a gift or kind gesture, your "You're welcome" communicates graciousness and ease and allows the other person to receive with equal ease and grace.

Croatian theologian Miroslav Volf explores yet another avenue for understanding welcome: the concept of *embrace*. In his book *Exclusion and Embrace*, Volf traces the four movements that comprise mutual embrace[2]:

- *Act One: Opening the arms*. This move telegraphs the desire to reach beyond yourself in order to connect with the other,[3] to be part of the other and to have the other be part of you. The act of opening your arms also creates space for the other to come in—boundaries are down, the self is open. Finally, he says, open arms are an invitation. "Like a door left opened for an expected friend, they are a call to come in."[4]

- *Act Two: Waiting*. You cannot force the other to come inside. You cannot reach out and grasp and coerce. You must wait at the boundary of the other, wait for him to open to you, hope that the power of your vulnerability and desire for the other will prove compelling, even transforming.

- *Act Three: Closing*. After the other steps into the embrace, there is *closing*. This is mutual indwelling, holding the other within the bounds of yourself and finding yourself received in kind. Such indwelling shouldn't be confused with disappearing, melting into each other or merging into undifferentiated beings. "In an embrace, the identity of the self is both preserved and transformed, and the alterity (difference) of the other is both affirmed as alterity and partly received into the ever changing identity of the self."[5] Nor do you have perfect understanding of each other; the goal is not to master the other, but to receive the other on her own terms and continue to seek relationship.

- *Act Four: Opening the arms*. Because the two have not melted into one, you may once again open your arms. Now you have the chance to look at yourself and rediscover your own identity, "enriched by the

---

2. Miroslav Volf, *Exclusion and Embrace: A Theological Exploration of Identity, Otherness and Reconciliation* (Nashville: Abingdon, 1996), 140–45.

3. Volf's use of the phrase *the other* here indicates the individual one who is not the self. It is not necessarily the outcast or oppressed other, as when I use the term. I have marked the difference by capitalizing the term ("The Other") when it refers to those who are part of oppressed or marginalized groups.

4. Ibid., 142.

5. Ibid., 143.

traces that the presence of the other has left."[6] And you look again at the other, the one whose identity will continue to change, the one who will continue to be both friend and mystery. The one you may embrace again with your now open arms.

This is the drama of reconciling, mutual welcome. Think of the times you have been embraced, welcomed, received. We all know how good it is to come home like that, even if the territory is new. When someone carefully, lovingly sets a table for us; when someone thinks of us and our needs and hopes; when someone listens with full attention to our story and then offers their own, without seeking to master or co-opt; when someone sets aside their own preferences in order to joyfully, humbly defer to ours. When we are welcomed like this, we can experience the state of freedom and love I believe God wills for all people. It is a joy to receive this welcome. It is also a joy to offer this welcome, to say to another person: "May I know you better?"

But there is more to radical welcome, as the word *radical* signifies. Radical, in this instance, should not connote the unreasonable, undisciplined action some people associate with the term. Instead, radical amplifies the welcome, broadening and deepening and launching it to the next level. It also indicates a deep, fierce, urgent commitment to some core ideal. That's not just any ideal, but one at the root of a tradition, a movement, and, in our case, a faith. As Bill Tully, rector of St. Bartholomew's in New York, told me: "Radical is Jesus. Radical is getting down to the roots."

If welcome is the drama of embrace, then a *radical* welcome is the embrace that is hardest of all, requiring the broadest extension and opening of self, even as it draws us back to our core values. It is the embrace of the marginalized, silenced, oppressed Stranger. "Here is the core of hospitality," according to Father Daniel Homan, OSB, and Lonni Collins Pratt. "May I know you better? Will you come closer, please? No, it will not be easy, but make no mistake about it, your life depends on this saving stranger coming to you and stretching your tight little heart."[7]

Who is this "saving stranger," The Other, who is at once a full, complex, individual human being with a unique story and perspective *and* a member of a larger group that exists within the social hierarchy, as we all do? It's best to take on this question in two chunks. Let's begin closer to home. Depending on who the dominant, empowered groups are in your parish, The Others are the ones you have the power to systemically marginalize and/or oppress.

---

6. Ibid., 145.

7. Homan and Pratt, *Radical Hospitality: Benedict's Way of Love* (Orleans, MA: Paraclete Press, 2004), 36.

They are, to borrow the language of the Visions Group, the *targets* of oppression, while those who hold certain privileges and power are *non-targets*.[8] It matters not what you as an individual feel you have done to The Other, or even whether there are particular ways you as a congregation have consciously hurt another group. Identifying The Other requires only the recognition that, within the social system in which we all function, some groups have been given social, economic and political power over other groups.

Now, we can widen the circle. Every church is a social institution, woven into a complex cultural and historical tapestry that operates beyond but has great implications for the individual congregation. So we all have to ask, "Who are The Others in relation to our tradition or denomination—the groups whose voices and gifts have not been part of shaping our collective identity, the ones who have not held much power or been welcomed with open arms?"

This level of discernment is crucial, if a little tougher to grasp. Suppose your church has lots of working class members; do you need to think about whether you're sending exclusive, classist signals? What if you're a largely black church in a multicultural neighborhood: why would you need to worry about radically welcoming blacks and other people of color? Why? Because when people who have been marginalized see the sign hanging on your door—Episcopal, Presbyterian, United Church of Christ, Lutheran, Methodist, you name it—they may automatically leap to a number of assumptions about who you are, who is welcome to fully share your common life and who is not. Despite your diverse membership, you may still be participating in many of the exclusive patterns of your tradition: music that is culturally limited, leadership structures that reflect the expectations of European, privileged, older, or straight communities, and so on. It takes extra vigilance and care to reverse the effect of the exclusive stereotypes and patterns your tradition has laid on you. It takes understanding who your congregation and your tradition have pushed to the margins. It takes a recognition of who is The Other and why.

Those are hard words for most of us to hear and process. If you're in a non-target group, you may feel the guilt and resistance creeping in: "I see where this is going. I'm now the enemy. Same old story." If you identify strongly with a target group, you may feel yourself somewhat objectified: "Surely I'm more than my group, more than my victim or oppressed status."

---

8. Valerie Batts, *Modern Racism: New Melody for the Same Old Tunes* (Cambridge, MA: Episcopal Divinity School Occasional Papers, 1998).

I can only promise you that this is not about guilt trips or victim complexes, but a statement regarding reality. We cannot transform systems without naming them. We cannot work for freedom and embrace unless we acknowledge what forces keep us from the reconciliation and compassion we know God is holding out for all of us. Part of what makes radical welcome *radical* is that it goes into the roots under relationships and systems, clearing debris and maybe even rewiring the motherboard so that we can live and welcome in new ways.

Radical Welcome Is . . .

How do all those elements finally come together at the congregational level? When I describe a church as "radically welcoming," it means the community seeks to welcome the voices, presence and power of many groups—especially those who have been defined as The Other, pushed to the margins, cast out, silenced, and closeted—in order to help shape the congregation's common life and mission.

Few communities could achieve the vision of radical welcome in its totality. Radically welcoming communities are the ones committed to transformed life, a life that aims to be:

- **Hospitable:** They seek to offer a gracious, warm space to all people, especially those who have been defined as "Other," systemically disempowered and oppressed, pushed to the margins. In the Episcopal Church and most mainline churches, that could include people of color, poor people, children and young adults, gay and lesbian people, seniors, people with disabilities, and many other groups.
- **Connected:** They link to their neighbors, to their neighborhood, to brothers and sisters beyond their neighborhood with whom they actively practice what it means to embrace and be changed by Jesus.
- **Centered:** They possess a clear, compelling sense of Christian identity. That self-understanding is based in part in their cultural and denominational heritage, but primarily in the unapologetic and clear call to live out the dream of God as they have discerned it in light of Scripture, tradition, reason, and their context.
- **Open to conversion:** They attempt to listen carefully to, make room for, share power with, and learn from groups who've been silenced, closeted and disempowered, and they are open to genuine conversion and transformation based on this encounter with The Other. On the ground, that means they allow God's Spirit *and* the gifts of The Other to enrich and transform their understanding of who is inside and who

is outside, what ministries they undertake, how they select leaders, how they do business, how they worship, what they claim as their mission and purpose, and how they partner with other groups.

- **Intentional:** They engage in training, research, active listening, strategic planning: some conscious, contextually appropriate effort that addresses individual, congregational, institutional, and systemic change. They realize radical welcome does not come merely as a matter of goodwill or a by-product of enthusiastic outreach programs.

- **Comprehensive:** They recognize that the work cannot be left to a specialized ministry area, like the Outreach Ministry, the Social Justice Team or the Hospitality Committee; it is a way of being, and should eventually be cultivated by the chief leaders through formation, worship, mission, and other areas of congregational life.

- **Becoming:** They realize this journey is never finished, so they are always becoming, always looking beyond the congregation to see who has been left out or pushed out, always aware that the stranger's face is the very face of Christ.

- **Beyond diversity:** They understand that radical welcome is not merely about diversity, evangelism, multiculturalism, inclusion, or getting it "right." It is simply, profoundly about being faithful disciples of the Christ who welcomed and still welcomes all.

- **Faithful:** They honor radical transformation not as a necessary evil or as change for the sake of change, a response to misplaced liberal guilt or a church growth strategy, but instead because they are saying "yes" to God's gracious invitation to welcome as Christ welcomes.

- **Compassionate:** They prioritize the work of creating "space for grace"[9]: small groups, forums and other settings where people can develop, express and hold their dreams and their fear of change, even as they deepen their commitment to radical welcome.

- **Real:** They acknowledge they will not be perfect or consistently, radically embrace every group. A radically welcoming congregation is one where the members are becoming God's radically welcoming people.

Radical Welcome Is Not . . .

As you seek to understand radical welcome, get crystal clear on what it is not:

---

9. A term made popular by priest and consultant Eric Law, whose works are featured in the bibliography.

- *Radical welcome is not an invitation to assimilate.* We must move beyond the traditional inviting church paradigm, beyond inviting people to come inside and take on what we've already packaged and nailed down (as you will see in part 2). We are offering an embrace, and that means we have opened ourselves, offered ourselves. The risk is great, but embrace requires us to gird ourselves with the love of God and to say, "Come, bring who you are. My arms are open to you. Would you open yours to me?" We will receive one another, not losing our unique identities and histories, but releasing the rigid boundaries so that our stories can connect and a new community might be born.

- *Radical welcome is not feel-good ministry.* We are not pandering to the self-centered consumerism or corporate, customer-service expectations currently sucking the life and gospel out of many churches. Radical welcome is not simply a matter of making new or marginalized people feel comfortable, fashioning church in our own image, or hopping onboard for the next cultural trend.

- *Radical welcome is not reverse discrimination.* There is no need to toss out the gifts of tradition, or to ignore the needs and voices of people who have enjoyed certain privileges. An abundant, radically welcoming attitude says there is room for everyone to be heard, and that there is something beautiful, valuable and holy that everyone brings to the holy banquet, including those who've sat at the head of the table for a long time. In reality, there's bound to be some relinquishment and loss on the part of the empowered groups, but only so that each group can speak and help to shape the community they now share.

- *Radical welcome is not a conventional church growth strategy.* You are quite likely to grow if you take it seriously. But that's because it is an expression of Christ's New Covenant, a way that is rooted in the gospel. Should you engage this transformation, others will surely find your community attractive and compelling, because they will see the passionate and compassionate spirit of Christ at the center of it, and because your hearts will be so open, radiant and fearless, they will prove irresistible.

- *Radical welcome is not political correctness or a haphazard, reactionary throwing out of the baby with the bathwater.* It is deeply faithful, deeply committed to welcoming and participating in the continuous, powerful, surprising in-breaking of the reign of God. It's about finding yourself utterly accepted and embraced by God, and then running into the world and your community to see how you could extend that hospitality to others.

Eight Radically Welcoming Congregations

I could tell you more about radical welcome, or I could show you. Here are some brief sketches from eight congregations trying to live the dream of radical welcome.

> We had to convince people that no one was trying to take over "their" church and run away with it. This isn't an "us" versus "them" situation. There's only us.
>
> ENNIS DUFFIS,
> GRACE CHURCH-LAWRENCE

Grace Episcopal Church in Lawrence, Massachusetts, was faced with that most painful of dilemmas: change or die. The historically white, middle-class city of Lawrence had shifted, and the sons and daughters of the aging white church community had moved on. Members of the dying church opted to live, and that meant embracing their now-Latino neighborhood.

From the beginning, there were concerns that Grace would become a Latino church, that the new members would actually "steal" the church from their white elders. The Latino priest and missioner, Ennis Duffis, took that fear very seriously. "We had to convince people that no one was trying to take over 'their' church and run away with it. This isn't an 'us' versus 'them' situation. There's only us."

Resurrection came when white and Latino members worked together to create and run several homegrown community ministries, and when they intentionally crafted opportunities to communicate openly and to truly enjoy and respect each other's cultures. Eventually, the dominant Anglo community began to welcome the leadership of younger, less educated, less affluent Latinos. Moving beyond mere representation, the thriving congregation now looks like the neighborhood: more Latino than white, including a Latina who heads the vestry and a Spanish-language service with praise music and lots of children, preceded by a smaller but stable Anglo service. The next frontier for Grace: continue to grow while nurturing points of common ground between the white and Latino worship communities and the ever-changing neighborhood.

> Jesus says go to the highways and byways and welcome those people. This church came to the byways and got me and showed me that love.
>
> JASEN TOWNSEND,
> ST. MARY'S-WEST HARLEM

Harlem, New York, is a mix of cultures, races and classes, and small but spiritually mighty **St. Mary's Episcopal Church** in West Harlem seeks to embody it all. A banner at the front of the church announces to the world: "St. Mary's-West Harlem: The 'I Am Not Afraid' Church."

The presence of white and black members who hail from Harlem's established middle class and from nearby Columbia University is no great surprise here.

Even the growing Latino population fits the neighborhood's multicultural profile. Perhaps most remarkable—especially for the Episcopal Church—is the leadership of the homeless and poor members, many of whom came for the community meal program downstairs and, thanks to the genuine and explicit welcome, made their way upstairs for Sunday worship.

These powerful apostles have brought a fresh spirit and urgency to the reading and singing of the gospel, and constantly challenge their companions' middle-class Anglican expectations. They also bring a commitment to welcome others as they've been welcomed. Jasen Townsend entered St. Mary's by way of the soup kitchen several years ago. When I met him, he was marching, shouting and waving as a straight ally in New York City's Pride Parade. Ask why he does it, and Townsend just points back to the gospel. "If the guests who were invited to the wedding feast won't come in, Jesus says go to the highways and byways and welcome those people. This church came to the byways and got me and showed me that love. . . . If you want to love Christ, if you want to live like Christ, then you've got to love every person." The next frontier for St. Mary's: broadening their radical welcome to include even more Latinos and lesbian, gay, bisexual, and transgender people.

Just blocks away, **St. Philip's Episcopal Church** in Harlem, New York, looks for the most part like what it is: the oldest black Episcopal Church in New York. Parishioners point with pride to their courageous founders, who in 1809 left the venerable Trinity Episcopal Church on Wall Street and demanded a separate home for black Episcopalians in New York. St. Philip's has been proclaiming black liberation theology ever since.

> We have a history of resisting oppression, but we also know we can't live off that glamorous history. Others need us. How do we support them, too?
>
> EMILY FRYE,
> ST. PHILIP'S-HARLEM

That venerable history drew the cream of black society for the better part of the last two centuries. But when Cecily Broderick y Guerra came to serve as their first female rector, she wasn't impressed. Instead, she said she sensed the church had become a "terminally closed system." So she set out preparing the congregation for transformation, both to welcome residents of their economically depressed neighborhood and to make room for gay and lesbian people at the center of their common life. She preached about the link between discipleship, welcome and transformation. Meanwhile, older black leaders began to make another link: the one between movements for racial justice and the struggle for gay liberation. As Emily Frye, a senior lay leader, explained it to me: "We have a history of resisting oppression, but we also know we can't live off that glamorous history. Others need us. How do we support them, too?"

Thanks to that welcome, a small, committed gay and lesbian community has grown at St. Philip's. Recently, with the support of the vestry and the Diocese of New York, the church became the host for Epiphany, the first Episcopal group for black Christian gays and lesbians. The church's leaders hope they can deepen the welcome to the LGBT community, drawing gay and lesbian people into parish leadership and encouraging members used to fighting for black civil rights to demonstrate the same passionate concern for their gay and lesbian brothers and sisters—and children. The next frontier for St. Philip's: keep moving on LGBT welcome while building greater relationship with the poor community that now dominates their corner of sweet Harlem.

> I think the cross over our altar says it all. You can't tell if Jesus is being crucified, if he's ascending or descending. What's clear is that his arms are outstretched to embrace us all.
>
> JOHN YORK,
> ST. BARTHOLOMEW'S-ATLANTA

Tucked away in the land of blooming dogwoods, **St. Bartholomew's Episcopal Church** in Atlanta, Georgia, is like a radically welcoming oasis. It bears all the marks of a healthy, suburban Atlanta parish—multi-building campus, more than 700 members on an average Sunday, thriving children's programs—and one mark you might not expect: the first out gay rector called in the Diocese of Atlanta. That move took a lot of guts. It also took plenty of preparation; the community's leaders had to carve out appropriate spaces for questions, storytelling, healing, venting, and even healthy departure before and after William "Mac" Thigpen's arrival.

For years, St. Bart's has made its mark by connecting with the people other churches might not, first creating a nightly shelter for homeless families in their own parish hall and then welcoming young adults tied to the nearby Emory University community for worship *and* leadership. Whatever they do, lay leader John York told me, they try to imagine how it speaks a fresh, liberating word about God. "We have this opportunity to say, 'Not all churches are like the one you grew up in,'" said York, a Texan transplant who grew up Southern Baptist. "I think the cross over our altar says it all. You can't tell if Jesus is being crucified, if he's ascending or descending. What's clear is that his arms are outstretched to embrace us all."

The next frontier for St. Bart's: extending the welcome and keeping people of color and people without the economic privilege most members take for granted.

St. Paul's Episcopal Church in Duluth, Minnesota, was once known by neighbors as "the fortress." Duluth's class stratifications run deep, and for most of the church's history, a spot on St. Paul's rolls went right along with a country club membership. Then the money drifted further east. Now

St. Paul's sits in one of America's largest poor, white communities, with increasing numbers of people of color only adding to the complex mix.

St. Paul's tried running from their neighborhood, usually preferring to "do for" their less privileged neighbors. The tide and the church's attitude have turned decisively during the last decade. But they did more than open their doors to the poorer and more ethnically diverse neighborhood. They opened the doors and *listened*. Then they set up or revamped their own ministries according to what they heard. Slowly, this historically white and wealthy church has opened its lovely, historic building in order to house homegrown social ministries and provide ample meeting space to a variety of secular community social services. As long-time parishioner Nancy Claypool admitted, "Some of us were reluctant to open to the neighborhood. We worried about stealing. We needed to go through some change to become a place that wasn't afraid of having 'them' around."

> Some of us were reluctant to open to the neighborhood. We worried about stealing. We needed to go through some change to become a place that wasn't afraid of having "them" around.
>
> NANCY CLAYPOOL,
> ST. PAUL'S-DULUTH

Now the parish is building unprecedented new relationships with its community, tearing down the walls so that neighborhood children and their parents can adopt the church as their own. They have vibrant ministries with young adults and are even taking steps to break through midwestern cultural silence regarding the presence of gay and lesbian people. The next frontier for St. Paul's: seeing to it that the poor children and families streaming inside during the week for various community ministries are welcomed as a consistent, empowered presence in the Sunday worship community.

Over the years, **Holy Faith Episcopal Church** in Inglewood, California, has bent and stretched to accommodate its Los Angeles–area community. When Holy Faith was founded in 1911, the church was just like its community: white, reserved and wealthy. In the 1960s, blacks swept into Inglewood and whites swept out of the neighborhood and, at a slower pace, out of the church. It took another two decades, but by the early 1990s, Holy Faith was half white and half black. Within a decade, Nigerians and Latinos arrived and made their mark, turning an integrated parish into a multicultural one.

> Please, preach in Spanish and then offer the English translation. It compels me to pick up a new language because I want to make friends with all these other people around me.
>
> DANIEL MOGBO,
> HOLY FAITH-INGLEWOOD

With every change, members have struggled visibly with racism and classism in order to incorporate the leadership, liturgical sensibilities and voices of the new community. Now they are learning how tough it is to keep performing the balancing act and to become a strong community (and not just several cultural groups that call the same building home). "The best times are when there's a combined service," Nigerian lay leader Daniel Mogbo told me. "I hope we do that more often. Please, preach in Spanish and then offer the English translation. It compels me to pick up a new language because I want to make friends with all these other people around me." Mogbo said they have to keep pushing, keep engaging other cultures and opening more fully to the discomfort of doing or hearing something new in the liturgy and leadership.

That's what they got when they called Altagracia Perez as their new rector. The first woman called to the post, Perez is Puerto Rican and black and fully bilingual. Her leadership is far from conventional, by design. "I try to bring a different set of questions. Not just how do we get more people, but how do we share power, how do you create a culture that is flexible and fluid enough to be open, constantly evaluating and reorganizing based on the reality around you." They will need those skills for the next frontier: welcoming the different socioeconomic backgrounds and cultures of their ever-evolving neighborhood.

> We've put so much energy into same-sex blessings and welcoming GLBT people, so now the boundaries are a little more permeable for everyone.
>
> STEPHEN CHENEY-RICE,
> ALL SAINTS-PASADENA

One of the largest, most visible, progressive Episcopal churches in the country, **All Saints Episcopal Church** in Pasadena, California, hasn't traveled an easy road toward radical welcome. On the surface, it looks simple. During the Vietnam War, All Saints served as a center for the faith-based peace movement. Throughout the more recent gay and lesbian liberation struggle, they have become a powerful voice urging the church to move from fear to hope.

Many congregations look to them for direction on how to step out on social issues while growing in numbers and financial health. What they could never face was the race divide.

Until now. Over the last few years, they've worked to build passion for the genuine inclusion of people of color, and to confront and transform systemic racism and classism throughout the congregation's many sub-communities. According to lay leader Stephen Cheney-Rice, that's the hardest work of all. "We've put so much energy into same-sex blessings and welcoming GLBT people, so now the boundaries are a little more permeable for everyone," he said. "Still, at base, people don't want to give up the goodies. There's still an uncomfortable feeling when they talk about race or class." Leaders have taken some bold, even controversial moves in order to jumpstart change at All Saints, and those efforts are finally bearing real fruit.

The next frontier for All Saints: continue spreading the critical conscious-ness within the congregation and building relationships in and outside the congregation, without losing their size and powerful voice.

At the other end of the spectrum stands **Church of the Apostles,** an emerging church in Seattle's funky Fremont District. COTA welcomes about 70 people to their main Saturday evening worship gathering, held at their arts-center-cum-worship-space, the Fremont Abbey. If you hadn't guessed, COTA is run by and for Generation-Xers (now in their thirties and early forties) and Millennials (now in their late teens and early twenties) and seekers of any age who yearn for postmodern, electroni-cally savvy, "ancient-future" worship, and radical, authentic Christian living.

> You can connect with people at a pub or a club. God has already been there. The question is, where will the church be? Jesus has gone ahead of us into Gali-lee. It's time for us to go out and meet him there.
>
> KAREN WARD, CHURCH OF THE APOSTLES-SEATTLE

Karen Ward serves as midwife and spiritual mother to COTA. She came to Seattle in the 1990s and sold the Northwest Washington Lutheran Synod and the Episcopal Diocese of Olympia on her dream: to create a Christian community for a generation of seekers who were wounded by the church or have simply never darkened a church door. Like others in the "Emerg-ing Church" movement, they are trying to get back to the source and create an authentic expression of church that honors Jesus' call and the church's ancient traditions and speaks the language of emerging generations and the cultures they inhabit. "Some people seem to think the Devil owns certain types of music, certain parts of the world, certain venues, and God doesn't," Ward told me. "Our theology says there's only one God, and God is already out there, everywhere. So you can connect with people at a pub or a club. God has already been there. The question is, where will the church be? Jesus has gone ahead of us into Galilee. It's time for us to go out and meet him there."

COTA has a clear vision and a strong commitment to building lay lead-ers who think of themselves as urban monks and apostles of Christ. The next frontier for this emergent community: convincing larger church bodies to invest in the church of the future, and convincing Seattle's secular culture that church matters.

✿ ✿ ✿

As you can see, radical welcome manifests differently in every congrega-tion, mostly because we all have different centers, different margins, dif-ferent contexts in which we operate. And yet, even as these congregations vary widely in their demographics, liturgical styles, social contexts, and even theologies, they share a hard-won commitment to open to the often painful process of transformation. They've sought guidance, engaged in careful discernment and offered each other the gift of patience. They've directed their energy outward—out to the community, out to God—and it has enriched their internal lives beyond measure. They've listened to each other, to their surrounding community, to the faithful witness of generations past, and then set a course for the future. God's future.

GO DEEPER . . .

1. Which of the stories, quotes or ideas you just read was the most challenging? Exciting? How do they connect with your own story? With your congregation's story? What do you feel inspired to ask or to do now?

2. What part of the dream of radical welcome sparks passion in you? Recall a specific story from your life that explains why you have that passion or concern.

3. What words come to mind when you think of "welcome"? What words come to mind when you think of "radical"? How do those associations help or hinder as you consider radical welcome?

4. When have you been radically welcomed? When have you walked into a place and found yourself completely appreciated and valued and included, despite your expectations? Reflect on that experience.

5. When have you felt left out? When have you entered a space only to discover no room for your voice or your identity? Reflect on that experience.

PART 1

The Theology of Radical Welcome

The Dream
of God

God is changing things so that they finally reflect
the dream of God. It will be new to us, but it is merely
the fulfillment of what God intended all along.

THE RIGHT REVEREND MICHAEL CURRY,
EPISCOPAL DIOCESE OF NORTH CAROLINA

Life would be so much easier—and church more comfortable—if we
didn't answer the call to become radically welcoming. Why would a community go in search of transformation and dissonance, when most of us
instinctively seek institutions to find stability and shelter from the storm?
Couldn't we trust that Sunday morning is destined to remain the most segregated hour in American life, that certain groups have mutually agreed not
to share spiritual relationship, and leave it at that? Why rock the boat? Why
cross boundaries? Why risk welcoming?

Earl Kooperkamp answers that question as well as anyone I've met. "Radical hospitality is one of the most important spiritual gifts," said Kooperkamp,
who serves as rector of St. Mary's Episcopal Church in West Harlem, New
York. "Look at Abraham and his three angelic visitors in Genesis. Look at
Hebrews, where they speak of entertaining angels unawares. Look at Jesus'
open table fellowship. That's my vision for what the church should be." Having
warmed to his topic, the community organizer-turned-priest continued, "Jesus
reaches out and bids us to do the same: to open our hearts and hands to those
around us, to embrace the abundant life that God graciously offers to all."

Why are congregations like St. Mary's becoming radically welcoming? Why
should any of us risk transformation? Quite simply, because God did it first.

The God of Transformation

From the beginning, God has been about the business of creating, reshaping, and making things new. The record of Scripture is filled with images of a God who turns things upside-down in order to get them right-side up, and creates something from what would seem to be nothing. Open the Bible to almost any page and you will see the evidence. In the beginning the Creator God takes the formless, watery void and brings forth life with a word and a touch. Later, we meet Abraham and Sarah, the unlikely patriarch and matriarch of Israel, both too old to expect to be the new parents of a great, holy people. Then we greet Moses, the stumbling, mumbling, ever-reluctant prophet and leader of Israel.

Online Extra: Exercises for Discerning the Dream of God

Though the truth and its implications are life-altering, can there be any doubt that God is a God of transformation who wants to embrace and transform all of creation? The promise is present in the prophet Isaiah, who cried out to the complacent children of Israel, giving voice to the word of God:

> Do not remember the former things, or consider the things of old. I am about to do a new thing; now it springs forth, do you not perceive it? I will make a way in the wilderness and rivers in the desert. The wild animals will honor me, the jackals and the ostriches; for I give water in the wilderness, rivers in the desert, to give drink to my chosen people, the people whom I formed for myself so that they might declare my praise. (Isaiah 43:18–21)

And in the closing chapters of the New Testament, we hear echoes of the same promise:

> Then I saw a new heaven and a new earth; for the first heaven and the first earth had passed away, and the sea was no more. . . . And I heard a loud voice from the throne saying, "See, the home of God is among mortals. God will dwell among them; they will be God's people, and God will be with them, wiping every tear from their eyes. Death will be no more; mourning and crying and pain will be no more, for the first things have passed away." And the one who is seated on the throne said, "See, I am making all things new." (Revelation 21:1, 3–5)

We humans might have a vested interest in depicting a changeless God who made a stable and unchanging world. Scripture, history and our own life experiences put the lie to that hope. "I am about to do a new thing; now it springs forth, do you not perceive it?" You have never seen rivers in the desert—this God will make it so. You have never seen wild animals obey—this God will make it so. You cannot imagine life beyond the old patterns and accepted ways that seem ingrained in the groove of creation—this God is not bound by those limits. This God is making a new heaven and a new earth, one where pain will cease, justice will rule, and death itself will die. God invites us to look around with the eyes of faith; then we, too, will see how God is "making all things new."

A warning: the new thing God is bringing to life is not "new" in the way we so often understand and fear it to be. Bishop Michael Curry of the Episcopal Diocese of North Carolina, the first black diocesan bishop elected in the South, and thus a man with long experience following the God of transformation, explained it to me with these simple words: "God is changing things so that they finally reflect the dream of God. It will be new to us, but it is merely the fulfillment of what God intended all along."

Many theologians have painted their picture of this new thing God is doing in the world, what Episcopal laywoman Verna Dozier calls "the dream of God" and what Howard Thurman, another black theologian and mystic, describes as "a friendly world of friendly folk beneath a friendly sky."[1] If it sounds pleasant and non-threatening, it is not. In his book *God Has a Dream: A Vision of Hope for Our Time*, Archbishop Desmond Tutu adds color, contour and depth—and teeth—to Dozier and Thurman's sketches of the divine dream:

> God calls on us to be [God's] partners to work for a new kind of society where people count; where people matter more than things, more than possessions; where human life is not just respected but positively revered; where people will be secure and not suffer from the fear of hunger, from ignorance, from disease; where there will be more gentleness, more caring, more sharing, more compassion, more laughter; where there is peace and not war. . . .[2]

Having labored under the weight of racial apartheid, neither Tutu nor Dozier nor Thurman was under any illusion that the kingdom had come, that the creation had indeed become some idyllic "friendly world of friendly folk." Their discussion of the dream of God hinges on their belief in a God who yearns for the transformation of a broken yet redeemable creation. "The world is not as God would have it be," Dozier admits. "The kingdoms of this world are not yet the kingdom of God, but they can become it. They are not

---

1. As quoted in Verna Dozier, *The Dream of God: A Call to Return* (New York: Seabury Classics, 2006), 24.

2. Desmond Tutu, *God Has a Dream: A Vision of Hope for Our Time* (New York: Doubleday, 2004), 63.

> Why do we do this? Because we're Christians. Christ ministered to all, and that's the model for me. He was healing and touching all people, eating with tax collectors and lepers. Our call is to be with all, too, not just where we feel comfortable.
>
> STEPHEN CHENEY-RICE,
> ALL SAINTS-PASADENA

yet the realm where God's sovereignty is acknowledged and lived out, but they can become it."[3]

In Jesus the Christ, we see the lengths to which the God of transformation would go in order to bring the dream to life. In the Gospel of Luke, the first act of Jesus' public ministry is to enter the synagogue and offer this prophetic pronouncement from the scroll of Isaiah:

The Spirit of the Lord is on me, because God has anointed me to preach good news to the poor. God has sent me to proclaim freedom for the prisoners and recovery of sight to the blind, to release the oppressed, to proclaim the year of the Lord's favor. (Luke 4:18–19)

Having dropped his bombshell, he rolls up the scroll, hands it back to the attendant, and takes his seat. Meanwhile, everyone is staring at him, at once aghast and in awe. He knows what they are wondering: Is this guy serious? His response is curt: "Today this scripture is fulfilled in your hearing." Yes, he tells them, the Messiah has come. The old order is passing away, and I have come to usher in a new age. Things are about to change.

And change they do. Jesus' whole ministry—the whole account of God's human life among us—is that of one who honors his tradition, but will not be bound by it if the dream of God demands something else. So he speaks to the Samaritan woman at the well, even though Jews and Samaritans were not to relate to each other, and especially not a Jewish man and a Samaritan woman (John 4:1–26). When he sees the man with the withered hand sitting in the synagogue on the Sabbath, he knows the rules: do not touch him, do not heal him, do not perform any unnecessary work on this day ordained by God for rest. He also knows he is being watched by the religious authorities who are waiting to pounce on him for the slightest infraction. Knowing all that, as Mark tells us,

> Jesus said to the man who had the withered hand, "Come and stand here." The man got up and stood there. Then Jesus said to them, "I ask you, is it lawful to do good or to do harm on the Sabbath, to save life or to destroy it?" After looking around at all of them, he said to the man, "Stretch out your hand." He did so, and his hand was restored. (Luke 6:8–10)

Jesus knew, and we certainly know, there would be consequences for his actions. He also knew he had come to do his Abba God's will, to usher in the just reign of God. And he knew, as we struggle to acknowledge, that there is no way to have the dream without the transformation. The point is not to

---

3. Dozier, *The Dream of God*, 106.

slog away in maintenance mode or to sit on the sidelines, pining for what was. The God of transformation invites us to "be glad and rejoice forever in what I am creating" (Isaiah 65:18). God yearns for us to be part of this new creation and to rejoice in its unfolding.

The God of Relationship

That invitation reveals another face of God. The Holy and Immortal One could choose to act without us, could choose to be the watchmaker who sets creation in motion and then walks away. But the very nature of God is to be in relationship, first within the Godhead, then with all of creation, and even with each of us, making us the very children and partners of God.

According to orthodox theology, the Trinitarian God is a God in *perichoresis*, or an eternal, continual dance, with Godself. The Creator is in union with the Redeemer who is in union with the Sustainer who is in union with the Creator—at all times and in all places. That relational quality propels God into creation, where God yearns for relationship with us all and draws us beyond our barriers and into relationship with each other.

In Scripture we see this God going forth, claiming Abraham and his descendants and establishing a covenant relationship with them.[4] That promise sustains the Israelites during their forty-year sojourn in the wilderness, and the Deuteronomist reminds them of the relationship when despair threatens. "It is the Lord who goes before you. God will be with you; God will not fail you or forsake you. Do not be afraid or be dismayed" (Deuteronomy 31:8). However dire the circumstances, however stacked the deck may be against them, they can always cling to the faithful promise of the One who speaks to them and has claimed them as beloved children.

Through the incarnation, God takes that intimate relationship another radical step forward. This time, God comes not only to dwell by our side but to share everything about our condition, surrendering the privilege of heavenly consort to take up a dwelling place within humanity. Some of the most beautiful poetry in the Bible is reserved to describe this wondrous moment, when "the Word became flesh and made his dwelling among us. We have seen his glory, the glory of the One and Only who came from the Creator,

---

4. I would add my own belief, shared with many liberation theologians, that while the Israelite story is foundational and formative for the Christian witness, God surely covenanted with many peoples in many lands at many times throughout history. For more, consult the work of Native American Christian theologians like Steven Charleston (see Susan Brooks Thistlethwaite and Mary Potter Engel, eds., *Lift Every Voice: Constructing Christian Theologies from the Underside* [Maryknoll, NY: Orbis Books, 2000]). The point is an important one as we seek to dismantle traditional insider/outsider distinctions, especially within Christian communities.

full of grace and truth" (John 1:14). Upon joining us, Jesus extends himself to humanity, yearning to know and be known, to have us join him in the divine union he has shared with his Abba God from the beginning of time:

> Abide in me as I abide in you. . . . As my Abba has loved me, so I have loved you; abide in my love. If you keep my commandments, you will abide in my love, just as I have kept my Abba's commandments and abide in that love. I have said these things to you so that my joy may be in you, and that your joy may be complete. (John 15:4, 9–11)

Listen closely and you will detect echoes of *perichoresis*, the eternal, interweaving dance between the three persons of the Trinity. The Son abides in us and we in the Son, who also abides in his Abba and thus allows us to abide with his Abba as well. The dance of embrace, mutual embrace, never ends. Through Christ, the relational God has grasped us, and we are inextricably bound up in the joy of the divine life.

Nearly two thousand years later, healer, teacher, social critic, and mystic Henri Nouwen summed up the mystery, power and call of the incarnation in these words:

> Jesus, in whom the fullness of God dwells, has become our home. By making his home in us, he allows us to make our home in him. By entering into the intimacy of our innermost self he offers us the opportunity to enter into his own intimacy with God. By choosing us as his preferred dwelling place he invites us to choose him as our preferred dwelling place. That is the mystery of the incarnation.[5]

> Grace is too good to believe. The world wants to exclude certain people, say they shouldn't be allowed inside. The church says, No one is excluded. We're radically open. God keeps getting bigger, and we have to expand with God.
>
> HOWARD ANDERSON, FORMER RECTOR, ST. PAUL'S-DULUTH

This is our God: a God who chose us as a preferred dwelling place and waits longingly for us to choose to dwell within God and align our lives with God's own will. This is our God: a God who yearns for relationship with us, risks everything for relationship with us, and finally dies to be in relationship with us. If we ever wondered or doubted God's yearning for relationship with us, the incarnation proves God's desire with humbling clarity.

Such incarnational theology is one of the hallmarks of the Anglican Way. The Church of England's first systematic theologian, Richard Hooker, boldly

---

5. Henri Nouwen, *Lifesigns: Intimacy, Fecundity and Ecstasy in Christian Perspective, as reprinted in Henri Nouwen: Writings Selected,* edited by Robert A. Jonas (Maryknoll, NY: Orbis Books, 1998), 5.

proclaimed that something of God is present in all life, and that via the incarnation we are indeed "partakers" in the divine life. "All other things that are of God have God in them and he them in himself likewise. . . . All things therefore are partakers of God, they are his offspring, his influence is in them."[6] For Hooker, this means we are at once held by God and the ones who hold God. The Almighty God has chosen to be in union with us, taking on created nature and in the process joining us to God's own life.

More than that, Hooker believed God has chosen to be vulnerable to us, chosen to need us, and even to impart a spark of the divine nature to us. "Sith God hath deified our nature (by the union confirmed through the incarnation), . . . we cannot now conceive how God should without man either exercise divine power, or receive the glory of divine praise."[7] God has established a radically mutual relationship with humanity, and based on those terms we are God's partners, the ones on whom God depends. Those are the radical implications of the incarnation, and they reveal the profoundly relational being of God.

God invites us to share in that nature, not only by some pure, mystical connection to God in Christ, but through our flesh, blood and spirit relationships with one another. At times, the church has conveniently interpreted this call as one to uniformity. If anything, what Christ came to offer, and died making possible, was union:

> [H]e is our peace; in his flesh he has made both groups into one and has broken down the dividing wall, that is, the hostility between us. He has abolished the law with its commandments and ordinances, that he might create in himself one new humanity in place of the two, thus making peace, and might reconcile both groups to God in one body through the cross. (Ephesians 2:14–16)

God rejoices when we move beyond ourselves, beyond our hostility and ignorance and suspicion, past our "dividing walls" and into relationship with one another, signifying to the world that we are one reconciled body, the body of Christ. In this, we reflect the mutual relationship and union that is the very nature of Godself.

The God of Welcome

Looking closely at the witness of Scripture, we see a God who not only seeks relationship and union with the creation but who reaches out intentionally

---

6. Richard Hooker, *Of the Laws of Ecclesiastical Polity*, V.56.5.

7. Ibid., V.54.5.

for everyone, and in particular for the outcast. Regardless of how unclean, unworthy, insignificant, or marginalized we may feel or others may claim we are, the God of grace and welcome shatters every barrier to embrace us and draw us home.

Lest we think the welcome is meant for us or our group alone, the Scriptures are filled with reminders to God's chosen ones that they are *not* the only ones God welcomes. In Deuteronomy, Moses speaks to the Israelites as they journey from slavery in Egypt and through the wilderness. The frightened, tired and confused clan no doubt sought comfort in the knowledge that their covenant with God made them special. They soon learned that there is no rest for God's chosen ones. Instead, God's people are called out for a special mission.

Online Extra: Bible Studies on the Biblical Foundations of Radical Welcome

> [T]he Lord your God is God of gods and Lord of lords, the great God, the mighty and awesome, who is not partial and takes no bribe, who executes justice for the orphan and the widow, and who loves the strangers, providing them with food and clothing. You shall also love the stranger, for you were strangers in the land of Egypt. (Deuteronomy 10:17–19)

It is true that God stands with God's people through every trial, but not so that they will sit comfortably with the privilege of apparent divine favor. Now they have to stand in solidarity with, graciously receive and *welcome* the vulnerable ones within their community and beyond it whom they might find it most difficult to accept: the orphan, the widow, the stranger, The Other. God has done it for them. Now they are called to respond in kind, literally imitating the God who graciously welcomed them.

Isaiah rails at Israel for trying to please God with superficial religious acts while ignoring God's yearning to extend justice and welcome. He shares this judgment as he has received it from God:

> Is not this the fast I choose: to loose the bonds of injustice, to undo the thongs of the yoke, to let the oppressed go free and to break every yoke? Is it not to share your bread with the hungry, and bring the homeless poor into your house; when you see them naked, to cover them, and not to hide yourself from your own kin? (Isaiah 58:6–7)

God has made it clear: if you love me you will work for liberation with the oppressed and marginalized in your midst, and you will share your home and food with those who have none. You will not hide from the brothers and sisters I have placed near you. Rather, you will actively go out to meet them and draw them to yourself, even if it is risky, even if you feel uncomfortable (and would you not be uncomfortable, after encountering the naked poor and welcoming them into your home?).

That message has certainly been muffled by people of faith over millennia. "If you are Christian," we say, "be kind. Give charitably. Serve the needy." Each is a noble pursuit, but they are *not* hospitality and welcome the way God does it. God's way is like Abraham, who greets the three angelic strangers at the oaks of Mamre with nothing short of reverence (Genesis 18:1–8). He arranges for their feet to be washed, brings them bread and an extravagant meal that includes the meat of a calf. He treats these mysterious outsiders like honored guests.

God's way is like the father in the outrageous story of the Prodigal Son (Luke 15:11–32). The rash younger son asked for his inheritance while his father lived, an act that, at the time, was the equivalent of wishing his father dead. Having squandered the gift and hit rock bottom, he returned in desperation to his father. By every standard in their society, and by his own internal moral compass, he had to know he was as good as dead to his family, barely fit to live among his father's servants. But the moment his face showed on the horizon, his father raced out "filled with compassion" to embrace and draw him in. I imagine the young man approaching, dirty and humiliated, head hung low with the fear of justified retribution and anger. Much to his surprise and our own, his father saw only a glorious face and a reason to celebrate in a wildly generous manner.

Henri Nouwen reflects on the meaning of this prodigal welcome for his own life, where he came to realize

> I'm very happy about having a gay bishop, radical hospitality and radical inclusion. But we strive for that so we can do Matthew 25:35: "I was hungry, and you gave me something to eat." We do it because we still have a dynamic sense that the gospel can change lives.
>
> BONNIE PERRY,
> ALL SAINTS-CHICAGO

> God is not the patriarch who stays home, doesn't move, expects his children to come to him, apologize for their aberrant behavior, beg for forgiveness, and promise to do better. To the contrary, he leaves the house, ignoring his dignity by running toward them, pays no heed to apologies and promises of change, and brings them to the table richly prepared for them.[8]

That is God's hospitality: the welcome that actively loves and receives us just as we are, despite every reservation, expectation or term we might set out, however strange we imagine ourselves to be, however far out we have been cast. That is Jesus' hospitality, as he illustrates with seemingly every action, and nowhere more clearly than in his radically welcoming table fellowship. He invites lowly fishermen, unclean prostitutes, marginalized tax

---

8. Jonas, *Henri Nouwen*, 79.

collectors, and insignificant widows to partake of the lavish feast he has come to offer all. And he does it to teach us a crucial lesson: God made us all and loves us all, and no one more than those society casts out or sets apart. There are no limits to the love and justice of God. So, now, having known the welcoming love of God, the Holy One seems to say to us, "Be released from your fear and scarcity, go forth boldly and share from the abundance you have received. Do not worry about who may be watching and what they might say. Do not worry about your dignity and do not set terms on your welcome." God has graciously, prodigally welcomed us, because it is in God's very nature to seek us out and welcome us home when we feel the least worthy of embrace. Can you do likewise with others, entering solidarity with the outcast you find yourself least willing or able to receive? Can you make room within yourself to receive The Other?

✿ ✿ ✿

Knowing God as the One who transforms, connects and welcomes does more than inspire us from afar. Why? Because if this is the nature of God, and we are made in the *imago dei*, then the same instincts are deeply imbedded in our very DNA. Some part of each of us surely rejoices in transformation, in seeing the creation and our own lives turning and turning in the direction of the dream of God. Some part of us must be made for relationality, made to be connected to God and to each other. Some part of us knows how to stretch in gracious welcome, to make room to receive The Other, to meet people where they are instead of insisting that they assimilate to our ways and meet us on our terms.

Such generosity and self-emptying are the marks of the divine nature; by the grace of God, they are at the core of our own human nature, as well. As we come to intimate knowledge of the transforming, reconciling, welcoming nature of God, we discover something beautiful about ourselves.

GO DEEPER . . .

1. Which of the stories, comments or ideas you just read was the most challenging? Exciting? How do they connect with your own story? What do they inspire you to ask or to do?

2. How do these reflections link with your church's story, or the stories of churches you've known?

3. How does this image of God as transforming, relational and welcoming compare with the God you grew up with? The God you worship now?

Living with Arms Wide Open

We have to lay down our preferences to make
room for someone else's. It's not about me.
Because of who we are as a community
you may need to lay something down on the
altar, sacrifice it. If you explain it that way,
maybe people will see that it's a privilege to let go
like this. You will be blessed in mighty ways
as your God gets bigger and bigger.

SARAH NICHOLS, ALL SAINTS EPISCOPAL
CHURCH-PASADENA, CALIFORNIA

On my desk, there is a sculpture of figures rising from a single root and emerging as three distinct bodies. Near the top, their arms reach out in a single embrace, one set of arms flowing into the other set into the other.

This image helps me to conjure the many movements of radical welcome. It starts with God's embrace of each and every one of us. It continues with our yearning to embrace God so completely we hardly know where we end and God begins. It manifests and deepens with our embrace and welcome of our brothers and sisters, especially those whom the mainline churches have found it hardest to see, hardest to touch, hardest to love.

This image also helps me to understand radical welcome as a spiritual practice, one that forms us more and more into the likeness of Christ and makes greater room for God to dwell in us. We cannot welcome others authentically and boldly if we do not see the link between that holy practice and the practice of welcoming and opening our arms to God.

] Surrender All

Mother Cecily Broderick y Guerra, the first female rector of St. Philip's Episcopal Church in Harlem, is walking with a congregation slowly learning to surrender to the God who constantly presents us with transformation and surprise. She arrived at the historically black church in 2003, but when I visited the congregation later the same summer, she was already preaching the gospel of transformation and stirring up a congregation comprised largely of financially comfortable middle-aged and senior African Americans. "You need to test yourself, see whether you're holding onto something the Spirit leads you to or if you're clinging to something because you can't imagine life any other way," she warned the congregation as she strolled the center aisle, preaching without text and looking into parishioners' eyes with a mix of urgency, patience, humor, and hope. "So watch out, because staying blind and hard-hearted can be an obstacle to your own discipleship."

> It's hard to get church people to do new things, to sacrifice something. I used to be like that. I spent my formative church years in a very rigid place. Then I realized I wasn't growing spiritually.
>
> IRENE MCKENZIE,
> ST. MARY'S-HARLEM

Reflecting at a quiet moment the following week, she told me, "A lot of people here aren't open to what the Spirit is dictating. They view the future by walking backward, and they have no tolerance for change. So I continue to reflect in my preaching that change is a part of life. It's not a reflection of failure. It's a reflection of being alive."

That's a tough gospel to live by. God knows we want to cling to something tangible, to stick with the way things have always been, to maintain traditional boundaries regarding who's in and who's out. But faith and real life come when we cling not to our own power or ability or institutions, but only to the living God. And sometimes the greatest blessing is that which wrenches our fingers off the controls and removes the illusion that we were ever in charge.

God has been calling humanity to risk and surrender like this for ages. We have already heard the bold witness of prophets like Isaiah, who shared God's plan to make all things new and God's hope that we would join that holy venture. Everywhere Jesus went, he held out his hand and said, "Drop your nets and follow me." He invited people into a life of abandon, a life of deep awareness and presence, a life transgressing boundaries the world constructs, and all in order to get to God. I can hear Jesus asking us now: "Do you think you know who's inside and holy, or who is outside and unclean? Are you sure what is pure? Are you certain death is the end? Ah, think again." He crossed lines and defied limits throughout his life—and beyond—to convince us that we could let go of our assumptions, expectations and so-called knowledge, surrender and rest in God, who alone has the final word.

Surrendering to God is not a benign act. Maybe that is because God is not a benign God. In a pastoral letter dated June 23, 2004, the Episcopal Church's then-Presiding Bishop, Frank Griswold, asked members torn by disagreement and misunderstanding to trust and not be "undone by God's wild and unpredictable ways." He continued:

> The love of Christ, given root-room within us, is a dangerous force. We know that—as was the case for St. Peter—love can take us where we do not wish to go. It can require us to die to our desire for safety. It can demand a relinquishment of our carefully crafted plans, of our fondly held views, and of our clear expectations.[1]

So much of our time in church is spent maintaining and protecting: buildings, doctrines, traditions, plans, expectations. God does not change, and the church—as God's people on earth—is not supposed to change. But what if that is not our call at all? What if, as Griswold suggests, the love of Christ is actually supposed to free us, to make us imaginative and resilient and fearless enough to go wherever the God of transformation would have us go? What if closing the door to change, something we might have done out of love for our traditions and communities, actually closes the door to the Spirit of God?

Benedictine nun and Catholic theologian Joan Chittister warns that church folk too often tip in that very direction:

> To close ourselves off from the wisdom of the world around us in the name of God is a kind of spiritual arrogance exceeded by little else in the human lexicon of errors. It makes of life a kind of prison where, in the name of holiness, thought is chained and vision is condemned. It makes us our own gods. It is a sorry excuse for spirituality. . . . The implications of that kind of closing out the multiple revelations of the mind of God are weighty: once we shut our hearts to the other, we have shut our hearts to God.[2]

---

1. The Most Reverend Frank Griswold, "A Word to the Church from the Presiding Bishop," June 23, 2004 (www.episcopalchurch.org/pbfrankgriswold/a-word-in-the-church). See Acts 8.

2. Joan Chittister, *Illuminated Life: Monastic Wisdom for Seekers of Light* (Maryknoll, NY: Orbis Books, 2000), 88.

Chittister claims, and I wholeheartedly agree, that there is a spiritual discipline in the act of maintaining a posture of utter receptivity and hospitality to new voices, new people, new ideas, new music, new words, new power. By opening our minds, our hearts, our very selves to The Other—the person of a different culture or ethnicity, the person of a different generation, the person of a different class background, the person of a different sexual orientation—we are letting go of our idols and practicing for that greater opening, the complete opening to the God who wants to be all in all *in us*. Being open, discerning God's presence in surprising places, is an act of love, surrender and faith like no other.

Saying "Yes" to Conversion

Practically every story in the gospels could reinforce this simple, freeing good news. But one need go no further than the first words of Jesus' public ministry, as recorded in the Gospels of Mark and Matthew. Jesus has just returned from his forty-day trial in the wilderness. He hears that John has been arrested and leaves his home in Nazareth to begin his work. "From that time Jesus began to proclaim, 'Repent, for the kingdom of heaven has come near'" (Matthew 4:17).

This word—repent, or *metanoia*—has a storied history in Christian tradition. Some translate it specifically relating to the confession of sin that comes before forgiveness. But in this instance, the meaning is so much richer. When Jesus cries to the crowds to repent, he isn't just demanding that they come forward and give an accounting of their sins. In *Welcoming the Stranger: A Public Theology of Worship and Evangelism*, Patrick Keifert borrows from New Testament scholar John Koenig to offer some useful commentary on Jesus' activity here. Keifert explains, "Jesus was calling people to a change of mind and heart in keeping with the coming of God's realm. The change, often called repentance, moved them from isolation to 'the fullness of community life which God had always intended for Israel.'"[3] Jesus is urging them, quite literally, to "turn around": to turn to a new way, a radically hospitable way that breaks through the old hierarchies and patterns of relationship in order to issue in God's new order. The call is to be converted, to be transformed, for the sake of the just, whole, loving reign of God.

Without a doubt, saying "yes" to God's invitation demands of us more than passive observation. We are not mere bystanders watching the

---

3. Patrick Keifert, quoting Koenig, in *Welcoming the Stranger: A Public Theology of Worship and Evangelism* (Minneapolis: Fortress Press, 1992), 66.

environment changing around us. Rather, God has promised: "I will sprinkle clean water upon you, and you shall be clean. . . . A new heart I will give you, and a new spirit I will put within you, and I will remove from your body the heart of stone and give you a heart of flesh" (Ezekiel 36:25–26). God wants to work *metanoia*—a deep, fundamental transformation—inside us. God wants to renew the creation, and that includes our very hearts.

Some people may balk at this image of a God and a creation that never seem to stop shifting. Is this all an elaborate justification for making change for the sake of change? Does this mean anything goes, that God revels in chaos? Absolutely not. For millennia Christians have spoken of God's plan to draw all of creation back into union with the divine will. That requires movement. And movement of any kind is change. If our natural orientation, or certainly the orientation of our institutions, is to resist change and movement, then something has to give. *Metanoia*—that conversion or radical turning toward God—is the necessary breaking and turning of whatever inside us is resisting the movement toward God. Our will toward stability can turn into idolatry, or displaced attachment to a symbol or idea that cannot possibly hold the fullness of divinity. *Metanoia* is the opposite force that frees our bound, trussed limbs for movement toward God.

> Let me tell you how much our comfort zones have shifted. People here used to say that anyone on welfare was bad. Now I go with people to pick up their food stamps.
>
> TERRY PARSONS,
> ST. PAUL'S-DULUTH

God needs a free church that defines itself as a community of humble, courageous, flexible disciples who are truly willing to surrender all. Why? Because God is a God of surprises, and our best posture in following and serving God is one of openness and receptivity. Every Sunday, in almost rote fashion, churches say "yes" to that invitation. We say it in the most commonly spoken words in the Christian tradition: the Lord's Prayer. "Our Father, who art in heaven, hallowed be thy name. Thy kingdom come; thy will be done, on earth as it is in heaven." Praying in the spirit of Christ, we beg for the courage, wisdom and humility to follow the One who surrendered his will and his life completely to that of his Abba God. We ask for the will to "travel naked into the land of uncertainty."[4] We say we want God to reign, want heaven to come on earth, so that the world might reflect God's will in the same way that heaven already does. That's a revolution! In this prayer, we acknowledge that the revolution begins with us, that God will have to transform our own will and then use us as instruments of the divine

---

4. Robert Quinn, *Deep Change: Discovering the Leader Within* (San Francisco: Jossey-Bass, 1996), 12.

will. As Christians, we claim we want God to be all in all. With this ancient prayer, we ask to be in sync with God, receptive to God, open to God.

Radical Welcome as Spiritual Practice

This statement places radical welcome in a whole new light. God wants to touch the places where we are brittle and make us soft. God yearns to release the latches on our locked doors, and to open us once again to the fresh air and surprising movement of the Spirit. One way that we experience this stretching and opening is by fully opening our doors and hearts to the people and cultures and perspectives on the margins of our communities. Our prayer is to be radically welcoming to God. We prepare by radically welcoming The Other, who is Christ's living presence among us.

That doesn't mean it's easy. Even for those who dropped their nets and followed Christ, the spiritual practice of staying open to God and open to The Other was far from intuitive. In Acts 11, some circumcised believers confronted Peter, frustrated that uncircumcised Gentiles had been accepted as part of the community. To ease their anxiety, he relates the story of his own dramatic conversion and opening. Once, in a dream, he saw unclean animals spread on a sheet coming down from heaven, and heard God commanding him to kill and eat the beasts. He dutifully replied, "By no means, Lord; for nothing profane or unclean has ever entered my mouth." The reply came from heaven: "What God has made clean, you must not call profane" (Acts 11:8–9). At that very moment, he awakened to find several Gentiles at his door, begging him to come and baptize a Gentile household in Casearea. He knew the message from God was about freedom: the freedom to go to this household, the freedom to trust that the Holy Spirit was already there, the freedom to be as radically welcoming as God.

> When are we going to realize that God comes to us in ways we'd never recognize? The Israelites thought the Messiah would come as a great military king. Instead, he came as a poor child from a backwater town. When are we going to get it? You simply can't place limits on God.
>
> GAYLE HARRIS, BISHOP SUFFRAGAN, EPISCOPAL DIOCESE OF MASSACHUSETTS

And so it is today. In practicing radical welcome, we ask God, "What would you have us do? Who would you have us embrace?" And when God presents us with a holy opportunity to be stretched beyond our comfort—either by welcoming a particular group or by allowing that group's culture and perspective to transform us—then we leap forward in faith, like Peter.

And like that great apostle, we will never be the same again.

We might think we are blessing others by this act of welcome. And, indeed, there are many of us standing on the margins of our own communities, wounded by painful forces of political oppression and left out by the culture and habits of mainline churches. There are so many people waiting for hospitality that is not conditional, not dependent on meeting certain insider terms and leaving certain parts of their identity and culture at the door. For them—for us—welcome is an act of healing and homecoming.

Almost as importantly, the radical act of hospitality can open and liberate those who have found safe haven at the center, whether they are European-American, economically comfortable, straight, middle-aged, or otherwise privileged. Most of us have moments when we are at the center, even if we identify culturally with marginalized groups. And those who receive power usually have to make a pact with the systems that secure our power, to cut off part of ourselves, to silence the voice that cries out for justice and relationship, in order to survive and be successful.

I know this because I, as a straight, able-bodied young adult who currently enjoys economic, educational and professional privilege, have only begun to reckon with the ways that I choose to welcome—or not welcome—people or ways that encroach on my sense of comfort or identity or propriety. And yet, whenever I allow myself to be pushed open, I find the act drives me back to my dependence on God, and increases my trust and love for the One who sustains me. Maggie Kulyk, a partnered lesbian with kids at St. Bartholomew's in Atlanta, has felt it, too. "I wish others understood that this isn't just about being welcoming, but that it's a way to deepen our own spiritual formation. We're not changing the music as part of a marketing campaign, but because we're inviting the Spirit in."

We can all open to God in this way. When we allow ourselves to humbly reside close to the heart of God, and our actions flow from that gracious place, radical hospitality will flow as naturally as our breath. We will find ourselves developing the compassion, flexibility, openness, discernment, awareness, readiness, and faith to be useful instruments of God's peace. And then we will discover that it is easier, even a joy, to open our ears and hearts to others and offer them a wide, gentle space to call home.

If we make such radical moves, we may feel frightened. God is waiting to receive us in that place of newness and uncertainty with open arms. We need only step there in faith. That is why theologian Verna Dozier defines faith the way she does: "Faith implies risk. I will cast my life on this possibility that God is for me. I do not have to have any proof except my commitment. I do not have to claim complete understanding—that is idolatry. The faith view of reality is frightening in its openness."[5] I love Dozier's frank words and the seasoned wisdom behind them. She is not fooled by claims

---

5. Verna Dozier, *The Dream of God: A Call to Return* (New York: Seabury Classics, 2006), 15.

that faith is about saying "yes" to certain doctrines, supporting the views of a particular church. She knows it is about going all the way with the God who transcends doctrine, denomination and tradition. She stakes her life on the God of transformation, relationship and welcome, the God who "calls a people to be the new thing in the world—the people of God."[6]

We are still human, so it does not work all the time. In fact, we are human and flawed enough that it probably does not work most of the time. But the good news is that one move informs and strengthens the other. I reach out in trust, openness and welcome, moving beyond my fear and closer to the one who is most unlike me; that challenging act of faith strengthens my mettle for the next leg of the journey and widens my heart. Likewise, when there is space for God to graciously pour more love, more trust, more beauty, more compassion into me, then I am more able to extend the same compassion and welcome to the world. It is the way of any spiritual practice. It is the way of radical welcome.

GO DEEPER . . .

1. Which of the stories, comments or ideas you just read was the most challenging? Exciting? How do they connect with your own story? What do they inspire you to ask or to do?

2. How do these reflections link with your church's story, or the stories of churches you've known?

3. What associations do the words *conversion* and *surrender* bring up for you? Are the words promising? Limiting? Confusing? Why?

4. Do you know someone who exemplifies this radical openness to God and The Other? What have you seen or experienced in this person's presence? What allowed him or her to live this way?

5. When have you had a difficult yet transforming encounter with someone who challenged your sense of comfort? What happened? How were you tested? How were you changed? Did the experience affect your relationship with God? If so, how?

6. When have you seen your church relinquish its carefully crafted plans and expectations? What happened? How were you tested? Did you change? How? How did the experience affect your faith?

6. Ibid., 3.

Be Not Afraid

The disciples felt fear, but that's where the Spirit
touches you. I've felt it like a presence. Every time
I step into a space that scares me, my prayer is
to make me transparent to the work God wants
to do through me. If I let fear cloud the way,
then it's getting in the way of the Spirit.

SARA HAMLEN, EPISCOPAL DIOCESE OF MASSACHUSETTS

Opening our hearts to God. Welcoming Christ in the stranger. It all sounds so holy, good and life-giving, so undeniably Christian.

It's also de-centering, difficult and downright terrifying. Make no mistake: Jesus asks something fundamentally dangerous of us when he invites us to follow him into the just reign of God, where we will have to lose our lives to find them (Luke 9:23–25). There is nothing easy or comfortable about losing your life, even if Jesus holds out the promise of new, abundant, better, resurrected life. We don't really know what that life will look like or what it will take to claim it. All we know is that our old ways must die, for there can be no new life without some form of death. Radical welcome is to a great degree the practice of embracing our inevitable fear of The Other, of loss, of death.

The Reality of Fear

Fear is as common as the air we breathe, the ground we walk on. Even the most daring risk-takers among us experience fear. It's simply part of the human experience, as Jewish therapist Miriam Greenspan points out in her book, *Healing Through the Dark Emotions: The Wisdom of Grief, Fear and Despair*:

Fear is as human as laughter and tears. Though few of us would care to admit it, we are all afraid. It gets down to this: the human condition is scary. Pain, loss and death are guaranteed the moment we are born. So, too, is some degree of helplessness in the face of apparently random events over which we have no control. We fear uncertainty, helplessness, isolation. We want to live without pain or death. And these impossible wishes make us all the more afraid. These basic existential fears inhabit us, whether we are aware of them or not.[1]

There is no way to avoid pain, and no way of avoiding the fear of it. Buddhist philosophy and practice begins with the statement of the First Noble Truth: "Life is suffering." It is not a pessimistic statement. It is a fact. Our many expectations will be disappointed; the structures that nurtured and supported us will suddenly shift; people and ideals will pass away; we will experience real physical pain. We will suffer, and we will not like it. We cannot talk ourselves out of it, and we certainly cannot shame ourselves or others into "getting over it," even if what we fear is another person or the change their presence represents.

Be Not Afraid

Fear is there, assailing us all in so many forms it can seem unmanageable. But the Bible's response to fear is clear and unwavering: Be not afraid. Isaiah heard that message, and as a result he wrote: "Surely God is my salvation; I will trust and will not be afraid, for the Lord God is my strength and my might; he has become my salvation" (Isaiah 12:2). The Psalmist heard it, and that faith inspired this song: "God is our refuge and strength, a very present help in trouble. Therefore we will not fear, though the earth should change, though the mountains shake in the heart of the sea; though its waters roar and foam, though the mountains tremble with its tumult" (Psalm 46:1–3). Jesus spoke these words as he prepared the disciples for his coming death: "Peace I leave with you; my peace I give to you. I do not give to you as the world gives. Do not let your hearts be troubled, and do not let them be afraid" (John 14:27).

Be not afraid. When the words or the message appear in Scripture, they usually herald some dramatic shift just around the bend. God's people are predictably confused, tempted to hide their heads and pray for the tempest to pass. Then God speaks a word—"Be not afraid"—and beckons them to continue on the path, and the story of faith lives on.

---

1. Miriam Greenspan, *Healing Through the Dark Emotions: The Wisdom of Grief, Fear and Despair* (Boston: Shambhala Publications, 2003), 169–70.

Alas, when we hear "Be not afraid," the gut response may be to assume fear is the enemy, a demon to be exorcised. Western culture trains us to run from our fear and other "dark emotions" like despair and grief. "The fear of falling into the darkness, of going down and not being able to come up, lurks right at the edge of our ability to feel at all," Greenspan explains. "Our culture reinforces this fear, which I call 'emotion-phobia.'"[2] We Christians make life harder still whenever we shove fear down while declaring that the opposite of faith is not doubt but fear. If we confess fear or anxiety, somehow that sounds like an admission that we lack the strong faith and back-bone of more mature believers. So we cover it like the dreaded scarlet letter that marks us as weak believers or bad people.

> Some people decide that change is worse than death. They're scared to lose control. They've so defined themselves as Episcopalian that the word becomes antithetical to change. They don't really know what it means, except that it's what they're used to.
>
> JANE OASIN, SOCIAL JUSTICE MINISTRIES OFFICE, EPISCOPAL CHURCH CENTER

Especially when the fear or resistance surfaces while we are engaged in doing noble, Christian work, it can seem nearly impossible to admit our discomfort. At the Cathedral Church of St. Paul in Boston, Massachusetts, where I serve, homeless and poor people are leaders throughout the parish and have claimed the church as their own. It is a fulfillment of the gospel vision. It also means many economically privileged people approach our steps looking for *their* Episcopal Church, only to turn away from the throng of unwashed masses who know this church as a sanctuary.

When I spoke recently with colleagues at a nearby church that doesn't open its doors so widely, they looked at me with pity: "Oh, you're the ones with all the homeless people." I was torn. Were there limits to radical wel-come, especially if it was creating this kind of press and causing others to find us somehow unwelcoming? What were the real costs of maintaining this gospel-based identity, and was I secretly scared of being further mar-ginalized by our association with the homeless?

My colleagues and I have wrestled with these questions, and I am con-vinced we are not alone. Of course, liberal Christians want to welcome *all* people at God's table! Of course we are willing to make *some* changes in order to welcome them. We congratulate ourselves for being so much warmer and friendlier than some other group or congregation. We say we do not feel awkward or anxious in the presence of someone who is oppressed and does not have the privilege and access we take for granted. We tell our-selves we would be overjoyed and pleased to have "them" as part of our

---

2. Ibid., 2.

> You're talking about asking people to get in touch with their pain. Well, we're not pain-seeking people. Never mind that pain is at the center of the Christian story. We want to get through the pain quickly and get to the joy.
>
> STEFANI SCHATZ-DUGGAN, ALL SAINTS EPISCOPAL CHURCH-BROOKLINE, MASSACHUSETTS

congregations (and declare it a shame that they do not seem to want to join us). No one wants to be a racist, a homophobe, a snob. No one wants to seem inhospitable in our polite church culture.

Meanwhile, we ignore the frisson of anxiety and the voice that whispers, "I don't know how to do this. I don't want to do this. Why are we going through this? God, why do things keep changing?" We keep silent, shove the fear down, pray for freedom from this sin. In one workshop, a woman admitted her desire to take scissors to her fear and "cut it all out." We want to clear out the evidence of our weakness, to deal quickly and move on, to use our rational minds and make sense of these nonsensical impulses. Then, we have been told, we will be free.

Except that the promised freedom doesn't actually materialize. Cut, and you only slice away at yourself. Rationalize, and the feelings remain. Deny, and the truth pops up in another place. If you have ever tried any of these tactics, and at some point all of us have, then you know they bring little more than short-term relief, if that. Why? Because, as Elizabeth Lesser tells it, "Repressed pain never goes away. It is stored in the heart, in the body, and even in the genes."[3] Repression, denial and silence are not the same as healing. The way of genuine transformation and wholeness—the real invitation behind the admonition to "Be not afraid"—travels a different route.

Buddhist teacher Machik Labdrön points the way with this refreshing insight: "In other traditions, demons are expelled externally. But in my tradition demons are accepted with compassion."[4] The "demon" of fear is not some external force. It is part of human nature, and thus part of our own make-up. What a gift it would be to learn finally to love what American Buddhist leader Pema Chodrön calls that "shaky and tender place," the place deep inside that holds our fear of The Other, our fear of change, and our fear of loss:

> Tapping into that shaky and tender place has a transformative effect. Being in this place may feel uncertain and edgy, but it's also a big relief. Just to stay there, even for a moment, feels like a genuine act of kindness to ourselves. Being compassionate enough to accommodate our own

---

3. Elizabeth Lesser, Broken Open: How Difficult Times Can Help Us Grow (New York: Villard Books, 2004), 62.

4. As quoted in Pema Chodrön, The Places that Scare You: A Guide to Fearlessness in Difficult Times (Boston: Shambala Publications, 2002), 49.

fears takes courage, of course, and it definitely feels counterintuitive. But it's what we need to do.[5]

Sitting in this way may at first seem self-indulgent and terribly non-productive. Then we begin to shudder and feel "uncertain and edgy." Difficult as it is, we have no choice but to approach the demon with care and kindness. If we do, Chodrön promises, the effect will be transformative. I believe that is because sitting with fear nurtures within us three spiritual gifts: wisdom, freedom and faith.

Fear and Wisdom

Fear is a wise teacher, and shoving it aside without listening actually places us in more danger, not less. As Miguel de Cervantes wisely noted: "Fear is sharp-sighted, and can see things underground."[6] If I fear walking around my Boston neighborhood after dark, it is because people have been attacked here in the past. That fear is smart, and should lead me to get a companion to join me for the walk. A friend was stuck in a painful pattern of dating women who expect him to be their caretaker, while they give him very little in return. He is wary now, checking for signals, asking better questions, sharing more about his own story and his own needs. His fear has served him well. Telling the truth about fear, no matter how ugly or vulnerable it makes us feel, is the beginning of wisdom.

Fear and Freedom

Facing fear can also make you free. My own spiritual and vocational journey has countless times brought me back to the place of facing my own stifling, confining fears: the personal, interpersonal, institutional, and cultural ones. I can hardly describe the rush of freedom and energy that surged through me when I began to walk toward those fears and toward the loss and pain that lurk in the corner of all fear. It's the difference between walking into the wind backward, and suddenly realizing that if you only step forward, the wind will be at your back and you could run. Or, as Elizabeth Lesser puts it,

> People love some changes. Give me that $10 million. Bring me the love of my life. Make me thinner. It's the painful stuff we run from.
>
> GREG WONG, U.S. DIPLOMAT
> SERVING IN IRAQ

We live in a river of change, and a river of change lives within us. Every day we're given a choice: We can relax and float in the direction that the water

---

5. Ibid., 9.

6. As quoted in Greenspan, *Healing Through the Dark Emotions*, 169.

flows, or we can swim hard against it. If we go with the river, the energy of a thousand mountain streams will be with us, filling our hearts with courage and enthusiasm. If we resist the river, we will feel rankled and tired as we tread water, stuck in the same place.[7]

Life experience has taught so many of us the same lesson: denying pain and fear only shackles and weakens you. Why not choose freedom?

Fear and Faith

When we stop running away from fear, we can experience true vulnerability, the sort that is only possible when you finally stand in the storm, lift your hands in surrender and pray that all is not lost. That is when God loves to step in: when we are at our most confused, our most desperate, our most needy. Like the disciples on a storm-tossed sea, we may grow frightened and fear the end is near. But Jesus walks out to join us with these words, "It is I; do not be afraid" (John 6:16–21; Matthew 14:22–27). Do not be paralyzed by your fear. Do not be consumed with anger. Do not get stuck on the defensive. Do not run from The Other. Our fear of change and pain is powerful and frightening, but Jesus waits to offer us healing and renewal, imploring us to keep on moving, promising we may be tossed and even broken, but we will not be overcome.

> People are afraid of change. Why? Because it's frightening. It threatens them. Who wants to let go of the things we find familiar? It's unfortunate sometimes, but that's the way humans are.
>
> MARK BOZZUTI-JONES, ST. BARTHOLOMEW'S-NEW YORK

In her book *Traveling Mercies*, Anne Lamott shares her own experience with being broken open by pain. She found herself floundering following the death of her best friend in the world and the end of a romantic relationship. Finally, in a passage I discovered soon after my father's death, she writes of what I now understand to be the grace of grieving and sitting with pain:

> The depth of feeling continued to surprise and threaten me, but each time it hit again and I bore it, like a nicotine craving, I would discover that it hadn't washed me away. After a while it was like an inside shower, washing off some of the rust and calcification in my pipes. It was like giving a dry garden a good watering. Don't get me wrong: grief sucks; it really does. Unfortunately, though, avoiding it robs us of life, of the now, of a sense of living spirit. Mostly I have tried to avoid it by staying very busy, working too hard, trying to achieve as much as possible. . . . But the bad news is that

---

7. Lesser, *Broken Open*, 237.

whatever you use to keep the pain at bay robs you of the flecks and nuggets of gold that feeling grief will give you. A fixation can keep you nicely defined and give you the illusion that your life has not fallen apart. But since your life may have indeed fallen apart, the illusion won't hold up forever, and if you are lucky and brave, you will be willing to bear disillusion. You begin to cry and writhe and yell and then to keep on crying; and then, finally, grief ends up giving you the two best things: softness and illumination[8]

Lamott's situation did not drastically improve when she began to face her own demons; mine did not, either. However, our ability to keep walking with courage, hope, wisdom, and compassion is incalculably greater when there is room for God to enter and offer us those two best things: softness and illumination. I do not believe God actively sends us trials to test us or push us into deeper faith. That said, I have no doubt that God delights when we turn, softened and broken hearts in hand, and beg God to be our companion in the way.

Practicing Resurrection

Fear is never the final word in any story with God. Far more often, the bold act of acknowledging fear starts a new chapter. For Christians, that is the whole story of the resurrection. We are invited to participate in Christ's death and in his resurrection, to let the power that destroyed death now free us to be the living body of Christ. Many churches attempt to bring this theology alive by placing the baptismal font near the entry, where members must walk by it to come inside. On the one hand, this move signifies that baptism is our entry into the household of Christ. But at a deeper level, we are reminded that we have been literally baptized into the entire life, death and resurrection of Christ. We are members of his body, and if it has been raised, then we will be raised, as well.

> "Be not afraid" is one of the most common commandments. God is trying to say, "Chill out. I'm with you." Of course we're petrified, but because God loves us, it's possible to go on, all the time, knowing God never leaves us.
>
> EARL KOOPERKAMP,
> ST. MARY'S-WEST HARLEM

That resurrection does not simply come on some unknown but imagined day when God will raise all those who have lived in God's embrace. It is a resurrection we can experience whenever we face death, all the tiny deaths that threaten to sap our souls. It is a resurrection that allows us to occupy a completely new posture in our daily lives. If death is not the end, if

---

8. Anne Lamott, *Traveling Mercies* (New York: Anchor, 2000), 72.

God's power defeats any enemy, including the most fearsome of all, then we can step forward and proclaim, hope, serve, and love without fear. Rainer Maria Rilke shares this stirring promise in one of his *Love Poems to God*:

> God speaks to each of us as he makes us
> then walks with us silently out of the night.
> These are the words we dimly hear:
>
> You, sent out beyond your recall,
> go to the limits of your longing.
> Embody me.
> Flare up like flame
> and make big shadows I can move in.
>
> Let everything happen to you: beauty and terror.
> Just keep going. No feeling is final.
> Don't let yourself lose me.
>
> Nearby is the country they call Life.
> You will know it by its seriousness.
>
> Give me your hand.[9]

Taking on the voice of God, Rilke urges his reader to engage everything life has to offer—its beauty and its terror, the changes and the losses, the joy and the pain—knowing that no feeling lasts forever. The pain will come, but surely it will reveal something of God to us. The grain of wheat will fall into the ground and die, but that is the only way for it to bear fruit. If we are not looking back at mistakes and pains or ahead for trouble and loss, then we find ourselves in a glorious, hopeful present moment, and that is precisely where the God of life waits to take our hand.

If we know ourselves to be unconditionally loved like that, if we know even death is not the end, Henri Nouwen points out, we are dangerously free to love and surrender all for Christ.[10] We can go anywhere, even if it means we might be rejected, even if it means we have to look deep into the heart of our own fear. We can go to the most terrifying place in the world, because we know we are "loved beyond [the] boundaries" of the world.

The words I hear when I imagine stepping into that place of terror, uncertainty, chaos, and fear—the words I hope you will remember should you take that step—are simply these: *Be not afraid.* You are loved. *Be not afraid.* You

---

9. Rainer Maria Rilke, *Rilke's Book of Hours: Love Poems to God* (No. I.59), translated by Anita Barrows and Joanna Macy (New York: Riverhead, 1996), 88.

10. Robert A. Jonas, ed., *Henri Nouwen: Writings Selected* (Maryknoll, NY: Orbis Books, 1998), 72.

are held. *Be not afraid.* You are God's own. *Be not afraid.* You will face your fear and you will live. *Be not afraid.* You have been called to live as the child of a radically welcoming God, to allow your very heart and mind to be broken open to make room for The Other *and* for God. *Be not afraid.*

GO DEEPER . . .

1. Which of the stories, comments or ideas you just read was the most challenging? Exciting? How do they connect with your own story? What do they inspire you to ask or to do?

2. How do these reflections link with your church's story, or the stories of churches you've known?

3. What kinds of change inspire the most fear, resistance or anxiety in you? Why? Consider the same question for your congregation and your denomination or tradition.

PART II

The Picture of Radical Welcome

Beyond Inviting and Inclusion

Our welcome can be a very surface thing. We said
we were welcoming everyone, but we weren't.
So the first five years of the Neighborhood Partnership
have been getting to know the neighborhood.
We didn't want to go out and tell the people
what they needed. We worked hard at not being
Lady Bountiful. People don't want to be projects.

RHODA ROBINSON, ST. PAUL'S-DULUTH, MINNESOTA

Lots of congregations would nod and cheer for the radical welcome
vision. Doesn't every mainline church want to be seen as friendly
and welcoming and to become more inclusive and diverse? Well, yes,
and therein lies some of the problem. Inviting is not the same as radical
welcome. Neither are diversity and inclusion. In this chapter, we will get
a clearer picture of radical welcome by looking at its cousins: inviting
and inclusion.

The Inviting Congregation

The inviting congregation is an admirable one: it reaches out, listens for
others' hopes and concerns, risks the possibility of
rejection, tells the story of God's grace in its community, and invites others to join it in ministry and
journey. It is intentional about evangelism (to draw

Online Extra: Best Practices
for Inviting Congregations

	Inviting	Inclusion	Radical Welcome
The Message	"Come, join our community and share our cultural values and heritage."	"Help us to be diverse."	"Bring your culture, your voice, your whole self— we want to engage in truly mutual relationship."
The Goal	**assimilation:** community invites new people to enter and adopt dominant identity	**incorporation:** community welcomes marginalized groups, but no true shift in congregation's cultural identity and practices	**incarnation:** community embodies and expresses the full range of voices and gifts present, including The Other
The Effort	Systems and programs in place to invite and incorporate newcomers into existing structures and identity; rejection or marginalization of those who do not assimilate	Stated commitment to inclusivity, but less attention to ongoing programs, systemic analysis or power; emphasis on individual efforts	Systems and programs in place to invite and welcome people, including those from the margins; to ensure their presence, gifts and perspective will be visible and valued; and to ensure that these new communities, gifts and values influence the congregation's identity, ministries and structures
The Result	Healthy numbers (perhaps with some members who claim marginal identity) but institution and its membership is overwhelmingly monocultural	Revolving door, with people coming from margins only to stay on fringe or leave; institutional structure remains monocultural, with some pockets of difference	Transformed and transforming community with open doors and open hearts; different groups share power and shape identity, mission, leadership, worship and ministries

new people), greeting (to help new people come inside) and incorporation (to draw new people into membership and deeper relationship).

We need inviting practices. Without them, the church is a stagnant gathering, an empty husk. Any congregation would benefit from an analysis to see if they are extending a genuine invitation, and commit to providing and maintaining that receptive space. If you're not sure whether you're truly inviting, consult the inventories and resources like Andrew Weeks' *Welcome!: Tools and Techniques for New Member Ministry*, Roy Oswald and Speed Leas' *The Inviting Church*, and a useful booklet from the Church of England called *Creating a Culture of Welcome in the Local Church*. In particular, Clayton Morris' *Holy Hospitality: Worship and the Baptismal*

Covenant[1] is an invaluable resource for assessing and then revamping your church's invitation on all fronts (it also includes helpful analysis from both inclusive and radically welcoming points of view).

You could stop there—isn't inviting like this enough?!—but I would insert a strong caution. Because as warm and attractive as it is, inviting generally assumes the existence of an ongoing, set gathering and says to the newcomer, "Please, join us in what we are already doing."[2] For our purposes, the key word when describing the inviting congregation is *assimilation*. Your congregation may be incredibly friendly, engaging and passionate, but you as the hosts maintain the option of remaining largely unchanged. The guest is expected to assimilate into your gathering or community on terms you have set, leaving behind his or her own cultural worldview and practices in order to adopt yours.

> Birds of a feather flock together. They also lock together. "This is who we are and we're not changing." I've felt some of that, felt pushed outside. You may not be white, but if you can "act" white, then you're in. It's a big problem.
>
> MARK BOZZUTI-JONES,
> ST. BARTHOLOMEW'S-NEW YORK

Assimilation is a tricky concept, because on the surface it seems far from problematic. Many church members I've encountered would argue (quite rightly), "As we live into our call and express our particularity, some people will feel drawn to us and others will not. We can't try to please everyone. Shouldn't we focus on maintaining a strong identity and boundaries? Isn't that why others would want to join us?"

The answer is yes. A clear identity and boundaries are important both to carve out and to maintain. You need to be clear who you include and who you exclude. According to Oswald and Leas,

> A Christian church usually excludes people who do not profess belief in Jesus as Lord. . . . But there are other boundaries that help us differentiate between "us" and "not-us." For example, some churches "exclude" those who are not comfortable with a certain kind of theology or those within certain socio-economic brackets (high as well as low). Some churches

---

1. See bibliography for details on each of these titles.

2. According to the schema designed by the Crossroads Ministry, a national organization that trains congregations and institutions becoming anti-racist and multicultural, a congregation at this stage is a "club." In other words, the community is "tolerant of a limited number of people of color [and others from the margins] with 'proper' perspective and credentials," and it "continues to intentionally maintain [the dominant group's] power and privilege through its formal policies, practices, teachings and decision-making on all levels of institutional life." For more information, see the "Continuum on Becoming an Anti-Racist, Multi-Cultural Institution," on page 70 and in the online resources section. For more information, contact Crossroads at (773) 638-0166 or www.crossroadsministry.org.

Sure, I get frustrated. They get one of us on a committee and say, "Generation X is now represented." It's the same with one person of color. Imagine if they said, "We can only run one white old man, or it will split the vote."

SARAH DYLAN BREUER,
EDITOR, THE WITNESS

exclude certain ethnic groups, others exclude those who don't include several ethnic groups . . . and so on. Boundaries are needed for a healthy church.[3]

And so, if you give people something clear to belong to, make it apparent who is inside and who is outside—including certain ethnic groups or economic groups and certainly other communities—then you will grow as more people come looking for their familiars.

The critical question I would pose to Oswald and Leas and anyone building an inviting congregation as previously described is this: a healthy church needs boundaries and exclusion, but are all boundaries and exclusions healthy or, more to the point, Christian? Is all growth a sign of genuine health? Resources like *The Inviting Church* and *Welcome!* say little on the topic. The Bible, on the other hand, says plenty:

> My brothers and sisters, do you with your acts of favoritism really believe in our glorious Lord Jesus Christ? For if a person with gold rings and in fine clothes comes into your assembly, and if a poor person in dirty clothes also comes in, and if you take notice of the one wearing the fine clothes and say, "Have a seat here, please," while to the one who is poor you say, "Stand there," or "Sit at my feet," have you not made distinctions among yourselves and become judges with evil thoughts? (James 2:1–4)

Exclusion may be necessary in the formation of any healthy community. But is a wealthy church drawing large numbers of other wealthy people and (actively or passively) turning away their poorer neighbors around the corner truly healthy? Is a white church to be commended for having little genuine appreciation for cultural expressions and relationships beyond their own group? Could these congregations grow in discipleship if they opened their doors and hearts to welcome The Other into their common life? Again, James is clear on the answer: "Has not God chosen the poor in the world to be rich in faith and to be heirs of the kingdom that he has promised to those who love him? But you have dishonored the poor" (James 2:5–6). Closing the door to the gifts and presence of the marginalized Other, even for the sake of clear identity and a certain kind of growth, may cause a congregation to miss a greater blessing.

---

3. Oswald and Leas, *The Inviting Church: A Study of New Member Assimilation* (Bethesda, MD: Alban Institute, 1987), 19.

Using the logic of inviting, we quickly find ourselves locked into a pattern of reaching out to people who will appreciate our institutions and practices *as they are*, or who at least seem willing to assimilate to them. If your focus is on invitation, it will be difficult to justify reaching out to those who are different from you. You may grow, and by most measures observers would call you healthy and successful. You must ask yourself whether you have answered the call to live as the whole body of Christ.

The Inclusive Congregation

The inclusive congregation is one that has heard and implemented some of the principles of the inviting congregation, and then added a crucial commitment: the biblical mandate to provide hospitality to the stranger. Whereas the inviting congregation's plan largely draws those who reflect the cultural identity of the existing church community, an inclusive congregation has begun to explore what it means

Online Extra: Best Practices for Inclusive Congregations

to welcome those outside their cultural group (as defined by factors like race, ethnicity, class, sexuality, and age.) They hear Paul's plea to "welcome one another, therefore, just as Christ has welcomed you, for the glory of God" (Romans 15:7), and they are getting familiar with and excited about the dream of inclusion.

These communities have the best of intentions, and many people may experience them as quite enlightened. What makes them inclusive instead of radically welcoming? The exchange is still largely one-way: "Come, be part of us, even bring your personality and culture because we find them interesting and exciting, but neither the institution nor the current membership will actually be changed or shaped by your unique presence or gifts. You may join us, but you will not affect our central cultural values and practices."[4]

As Sheryl Kujawa-Holbrook explains in her study of multiracial congregations, the core problem is that the inclusive church has yet to really address power. (While she emphasizes racial dynamics, her analysis and definitions are eminently transferable.) She defines power as "the

---

4. According to the Crossroads schema, a congregation like this is interested in symbolic or even identity change: members make official policy statements on diversity and even cultivate a growing awareness of the systemic nature of racism. They include members of the marginalized group(s) on some committees or on the staff. However, they draw the line at welcoming people who "make waves" and leave essentially intact the institutional structures and culture that maintain [the dominant group's] power and privilege. See their resource on page 70.

> They say come, but they don't want you to make an impact. You're welcome— to become one of us.
>
> RUY COSTA, EPISCOPAL CITY MISSION, EPISCOPAL DIOCESE OF MASSACHUSETTS

capacity to have control, authority or influence over others. . . . Social power refers to the capacity of dominant (white) culture to have control, authority and influence over people of color. Social power plus prejudice equals oppression."[5] Many churches send members to anti-racism or other anti-oppression trainings, hoping they will come back transformed people. Only a tiny group of those communities move past the analysis of individual and interpersonal attitudes and behaviors to address the structural supports for oppression and dominance. If anything, Kujawa-Holbrook argues, "most religious institutions stop or drastically curtail antiracism efforts that move beyond personal and interpersonal awareness of racism."[6] Put bluntly, they didn't sign on for that level of transformation. They didn't open the door to share power.

These congregations are striving to be genuinely hospitable and inclusive, but the operative word to describe their goal is really *incorporation*, offering marginalized people a place inside, but still on terms that allow the hosting institution's power structures and identity to remain unchanged. So while they are open in theory and ideology, and they often thrill at the presence of a person of color or a gay or lesbian person or young adult or (more rarely) a person who appears to be poor or homeless,

- They incorporate different cultures into their worship, but without building relationships or sustaining an effort to educate and excite the larger community about the impact of fresh voices and perspectives. It stays at the level of "cultural tourism."
- They may open their doors to marginalized groups, but that invitation usually goes out to certain, acceptable members of the marginal group, often the ones who share the dominant group's class, culture, or aesthetic values (e.g., black Ivy League graduates, gay bankers, young classical music lovers, articulate homeless people, and so on). These members can be trusted as leaders. Other more marginal representatives likely won't get that welcome.
- They may partner with "diverse" congregations, but usually the "haves" are offering something to those who "have not." The church's ministries foster the assumption that certain groups are the objects of service

5. Kujawa-Holbrook, *A House of Prayer for All Peoples: Building Multiracial Community* (Bethesda, MD: Alban Institute, 2004), 15.

6. Ibid., 22.

but not subjects with whom they engage in genuine partnership and embrace. Mutuality and interdependence has yet to break in and transform these relationships.

Thus, the inclusive church's culture and environment will continually contradict its warm welcome. "Come in and join us, and please come back!" members say with their lips. But they wind up creating a revolving door, promising to receive people whom they have yet to develop the capacity to truly welcome.

> I heard someone say, "Anyone who wants to come to this church would be welcome; why do we have to make a statement?" We had to explain that some people would never cross that threshold.
>
> LUCIE THOMAS, ST. PAUL'S-DULUTH

The inclusive stage is vital in a congregation's journey. Many churches reach this point and stay, because they are not prepared to release control and surrender the tight hold on their established identity and practices. Others may begin with inclusion, only to hit the wall or notice the revolving door through which marginalized people tend to travel. This dissonant awareness causes a fissure, and that break lets light stream in from the other side. That's how you know there's more to do, further to go. That's how many churches arrive at radical welcome.

The Radically Welcoming Congregation

Radical welcome takes us to the root level, the Jesus-level. It understands that a church needs to have a clear identity, mission and purpose, and it finds its *raison d'etre* in the good news of liberation, justice and reconciliation for all of creation. Thus rooted, radically welcoming communities can go forth in Christian mission and ask the hard question: Who is not at the table? Who would never even come to the door because they are so sure we will not receive them, because, historically, we have not?

Those outsiders may be people of color, poor people, young adults, gay, lesbian, bisexual and transgendered people. They may be children, people with mental or physical disabilities, the homeless, addicts, ex-offenders, or the elderly (especially those without financial means). They may actually be represented in the community, but they have yet to engage significantly at the deepest levels of parish life and leadership. And they may have lived near the church their whole lives and been told your church is one of *those* churches. Like Tony LeDeaux, an American

> First it's about getting people onto the same page, that you can't be Christian without being welcoming. That being a country club might be socially acceptable, but it's not what Jesus wanted.
>
> LALTAGRACIA PEREZ,
> HOLY FAITH-INGLEWOOD

Continuum on Becoming an

MONOCULTURAL ➡		MULTICULTURAL ➡
Racial and Cultural Differences Seen as Defects		**Tolerant of Racial and . . .**
1. Exclusive A Segregated Institution	**2. Passive** A "Club" Institution	**3. Symbolic Change** A Multicultural Institution
• Intentionally and publicly excludes or segregates African Americans, Native Americans, Latinos and Asian Americans • Intentionally and publicly enforces the racist status quo throughout institution • Institutionalization of racism includes formal policies and practices, teachings and decision-making on all levels • Usually has similar intentional policies and practices toward other socially oppressed groups, such as women, disabled, elderly and children, lesbians and gays, Third World citizens, etc.	• Tolerant of a limited number of People of Color with "proper" perspective and credentials • May still secretly limit or exclude People of Color in contradiction to public policies • Continues to intentionally maintain white power and privilege through its formal policies and practices, teachings and decision-making on all levels of institutional life • Often declares, "We don't have a problem."	• Makes official policy pronouncements regarding multicultural diversity • Sees itself as "non-racist" institution with open doors to People of Color • Carries out intentional inclusiveness efforts, recruiting "someone of color" on committees or office staff • Expanding view of diversity includes other socially oppressed groups, such as women, disabled, elderly and children, lesbians and gays, Third World citizens, etc. But . . . • "Not those who make waves" • Little or no contextual change in culture, policies and decision-making • Is still relatively unaware of continuing patterns of privilege, paternalism and control

Anti-Racist, Multicultural Institution

ANTI-RACIST ➡	ANTI-RACIST MULTICULTURAL	
Cultural Differences	**Racial and Cultural Differences Seen as Assets**	
4. Identity Change An Anti-Racist Institution	**5. Structural Change** A Transforming Institution	**6. Fully Inclusive** A Transformed Institution in a Transformed Society
• Growing understanding of racism as barrier to effective diversity • Develops analysis of systemic racism • Sponsors programs of anti-racism training • New consciousness of institutionalized white power and privilege • Develops intentional identity as an "anti-racist" institution • Begins to develop accountability to racially oppressed communities • Increasing commitment to dismantle racism and eliminate inherent white advantage But . . . • Institutional structures and culture that maintain white power and privilege still intact and relatively untouched	• Commits to process of intentional institutional restructuring, based on anti-racist analysis and identity • Audits and restructures all aspects of institutional life to ensure full participation of People of Color, including their worldview, culture and lifestyles • Implements structures, policies and practices with inclusive decision-making and other forms of power sharing on all levels of the institution's life and work • Commits to struggle to dismantle racism in the wider community, and builds clear lines of accountability to racially oppressed communities • Anti-racist multicultural diversity becomes an institutionalized asset • Redefines and rebuilds all relationships and activities in society, based on anti-racist commitments	• Future vision of an institution and wider community that has overcome systemic racism • Institution's life reflects full participation and shared power with diverse racial, cultural and economic groups in determining its mission, structure, constituency, policies and practices • Full participation in decisions that shape the institution, and inclusion of diverse cultures, lifestyles and interests • A sense of restored community and mutual caring • Allies with others in combating all forms of social oppression

> The whole idea of hospitality has to do with accepting people where they are. We usually show them our books, and then get annoyed if they're not as excited as we are. We don't say, "What are your gifts? Your questions?" Maybe in a token way we put them on a committee, as long as it's not Finance or the Altar Guild.
>
> JANE OASIN, SOCIAL JUSTICE MINISTRIES OFFICE, EPISCOPAL CHURCH CENTER

Indian lay leader at St. Paul's-Duluth, they've seen the signs. "In the Indian community, we know about the Episcopal Church. It's got a big sign outside that says, 'Whites Only.'" To be truly welcomed, they need to see the signs of genuine openness and not mere tolerance. They need to know that they matter and that they can bring their whole selves into church, and *not* only so that they can be assimilated into the church's dominant culture.

The movement from inviting to inclusion to radical welcome is the move toward cultivating mutually transforming relationship. The terms and power have shifted. Both parties matter, and both are open to conversion. People on the margins will enter and discover resonances, time-honored wisdom and beauty in the congregation's received tradition, even as they share love and stories and engage in ministry as part of the gathered body. But the existing community will also experience conversion, hearing with new ears the wisdom brothers or sisters bring from the margins, trying on new practices, engaging God from a different perspective, and expanding their sense of what is possible, normative, essential, or holy for Christian life in their context. Structures are changing, and lives are changing, as well.[7]

If invitation is assimilation, and inclusion is incorporation, then the key word for radical welcome is *incarnation*. Jesus emptied himself and took on humanity; radical welcome calls us to surrender and openness to the culture and perspective of The Other. You should not release your heritage wholesale or attempt to erase everything and start from scratch. You need not demonize the gifts of the dominant culture. But you will have to examine the elements of your church life—your mission, identity, liturgy, leadership, and ministries—and determine where there is more flexibility than you first thought, which supposed essentials and non-negotiables are in fact simply your preferences, where you might be able to make room for another voice

---

7. Crossroads defines congregations at this stage as either "transforming" or "transformed," working for structural change in order to become fully inclusive. By transforming, they are actively, strategically rebuilding their congregational life and the wider society in concert with a multicultural, anti-racist vision. The fully realized vision is a transformed congregation, one where people once on the margins are fully enfranchised, where the church reflects "full participation and shared power with diverse racial, cultural, and economic groups in determining its mission, structure, constituency, policies, and practices," and where the congregation is actively working to eliminate oppression in the wider world. See the Crossroads resource on pages 70 to 71 of this chapter.

or perspective to enrich, enhance, stand alongside, and even transform the one generally privileged. As the seminal report from the Church of England, *Mission-Shaped Church: Church Planting and Fresh Expressions of Church in a Changing Context*,[8] makes clear, we must learn to listen, surrender, and immerse ourselves in the wisdom of the gospel and in our cultural context. We do it for the sake of the Incarnate One, Jesus the Christ.

Priest and consultant Caroline Fairless understands how easy it is to stop before delving into the hard work of radical welcome, but she urges communities to plunge into these deeper waters:

> The common language we use to evangelize is so often the language of coercion rather than conversion. We welcome you. We want you. Be like us. We do it to our children. We do it to each other. Can we reach for a vision of evangelism that assumes that each new person who graces the community will alter the complexion and the spirituality and the depths of the community? Can we understand this as a good and desirable thing? Can we understand evangelism in terms of the mutuality of the exchange of the gospel?[9]

What if we began to understand that kind of mutually transforming exchange of the gospel as a central part of our mission as Christian communities? It would profoundly shift the starting ground for congregational development. On the one hand, the radically welcoming congregation should do much of the same work that the inviting or welcoming church would; gospel-centered, structural transformation is crucial, but don't neglect the importance of an attractive website that tells your story and a clear process for incorporating new people into your common life. The difference is that radically welcoming communities look at conventional congregational development strategies and then ask the hard questions about who's inside, who's outside and what it would take to go beyond inclusion to mutual embrace and transformation.

GO DEEPER . . .

1. Which of the stories, comments or ideas you just read was the most challenging? Exciting? How do they connect with your own story? What do they inspire you to ask or to do?

---

8. Archbishop's Council, *Mission-Shaped Church: Church Planting and Fresh Expressions of Church in a Changing Context* (London: Church House Publishing, 2004).

9. Caroline Fairless, *Children at Worship—Congregations in Bloom* (New York: Church Publishing Inc., 2000), 148.

2. How do these reflections link with your church's story, or the stories of churches you've known?

3. Take another look at the "Inviting/Inclusive/Radical Welcome" table on page 64. Which of these models best fits your church's operative ideal (where you are headed, unless there is a change of direction)? What observations bring you to that conclusion? If you're headed to inviting or inclusion but dream of radical welcome, what could you do to help your community to change course?

Radical Welcome Signs

We have about 120 people here every Tuesday night
for a Community Kitchen, our version of a Soup Kitchen.
There's great conversation and a meal. So when our associate
Bridget was ordained, she invited a whole bunch
of that crew to the service. They came to the church then, and
they're still coming. We had a Newcomers' party,
and they parked their baskets right next to someone's
Subaru and came right in. Now, I know there's still
classism out there. But I've never seen people
crossing boundaries like this. It's a profound thing
to see the gospel lived out. It gets you excited.

BONNIE PERRY, ALL SAINTS-CHICAGO

If you were hunting for an Episcopal church in an unfamiliar neighborhood, you might look for the ubiquitous sign announcing "The Episcopal Church Welcomes You!" How do you know when you've found a radically welcoming church? What are the visible signs that a community is opening its doors and its common life to The Other?

I've grouped these signs, or criteria, into five categories[1]: mission and vision, identity, ministries and relationships, leadership and feedback

---

1. Many thanks to my colleagues on the Diocese of Massachusetts' Congregational Development and Support Team. Their work to set out criteria for vital congregations helped me to organize this schema for describing radically welcoming congregations.

systems, and worship. The point is not whether a congregation has achieved them all. These criteria can give us a clear vision and attainable goals to reach for and imagine with.

Mission and Vision

1. A clear, compelling, transformational mission and vision—one that incorporates radical welcome of The Other—has been discerned, communicated and supported by the community.
2. The mission and vision guide the continuing development of the community's identity, ministries, leadership, and worship.

Identity

1. The congregation values its history, traditions and denominational heritage; it also fosters an identity flexible enough to include The Other.
2. Leaders have consciously studied the make-up of the surrounding community and intentionally invited those neighbors to join and help to shape their common life and common mission.
3. The congregation is developing critical consciousness of who is inside, who is marginalized and who is outside, and why, and seeks to eliminate exclusionary barriers blocking The Other.

Ministries and Relationships

1. The congregation's activities have been thoughtfully organized to reflect and fulfill the radically welcoming mission.
2. Community ministries reflect mutuality and a desire for empowerment and transformation of self, other and community (doing *with* others, rather than doing *for* others).
3. Ministries draw members at the community's center and its margins into mutual, transforming relationship.

Leadership and Feedback Systems

1. Leaders are intentionally recruited, mentored and selected from the distinct groups in the community, with special attention to building power among the under-represented margins.
2. There is wide access to decision-makers and transparency regarding decision-making.
3. Different cultural and generational styles of leadership are understood and creatively accommodated.

Worship

1. The make-up of the worshiping body—which may be spread over more than one service—reflects the surrounding community.

2. Liturgical texts, music, images, and worship leaders reflect the congregation and surrounding community.

3. The community's worship is lively and reflective, deeply rooted in lived traditions, yet open to fresh expressions (again, not necessarily in a single service).

Focusing in these areas, it's a lot easier to explore at greater depth what the radically welcoming dream of God looks like when it's made incarnate in real congregations.[2]

Mission and Vision

What Is It?   The congregation's understanding of its purpose and direction as the radically welcoming people of God in the long- and short-term.

The Signs: 1. A clear, compelling, transformational mission and vision— one that incorporates radical welcome of The Other—has been discerned, communicated and supported by the community.

2. The mission and vision guide the continuing development of the community's identity, ministries, leadership, and worship.

If anyone is wondering what the reign of God looks like, they should be able to look at the mission of the church and catch a glimpse. As the Catechism in the Book of Common Prayer (BCP) reminds Episcopalians, our mission as church is to "restore all people to unity with God and each other in Christ."[3] We are the reconcilers who go forth, forge redeeming and reconciling relationships in the world God made, and bring the creation home to God.

At St. Bartholomew's in Atlanta, that calling translates into a radical mission, particularly down South. Their mission statement, printed in a variety of visible places and referenced regularly by leaders, reads as follows: "We open our doors to all who seek God or a deeper knowledge of God. We are a nurturing, inclusive community centered in Jesus Christ, called to grow in our faith through worship, ministry, education, and service." It's not a sexy

---

2. Looking for even more compelling visions to inspire your community? Consult the bibliography for resources.

3. BCP, 855.

statement, but over the years, that commitment has led them to open their parish hall to homeless families six nights a week in a program conceived, organized and run by parishioners (and this during an interim period!). It has led them to reconfigure their leadership structures and demands so that students and other young adults ordinarily perceived as transitory and pushed to the margins could take full part in the life of the community (why require young, new members of the Altar Guild to do every task for an entire week, when you could break up the tasks for those who might be working or studying?). Most recently, it opened the way for them to call Mac Thigpen as their rector.

"Calling a gay rector made us vulnerable," said the Reverend Charles Geary, a deacon who serves on the St. Bartholomew's staff. "I was the coordinator for Toco Hills Ministry (a collective of neighborhood social ministries), and we had a broad spectrum of conservative churches and excellent relations. After Mac was called, the Baptists left, all because he's gay. So yes, there have been repercussions." Invitations to ecumenical events stopped coming and local conservative leaders protested. LGBT people might not have become the majority, but St. Bartholomew's was definitely known as the "gay" church.

> I took a van full of students to different congregations all over town on Sundays. It was amazing to arrive with this group, identifiably undergrads, and nobody would speak to us. St. Bart's was the only one where people came up and were excited about this group of young people.
>
> NANCY BAXTER,
> ST. BARTHOLOMEW'S-ATLANTA

Then something happened. The crisis pushed them to clarify their radically welcoming mission. They redoubled their focus on welcome for *all* people, taking more care to follow up with visitors, hoping that for every person who left or was scared off, there would be more who were curious and even excited about this risk-taking church. Monthly dinner groups gather a mix of members—young adults and elders, gay and straight, old-timers and newcomers—as they work hard to keep the community integrated and vibrant.

The call to join gay and lesbian people on the margins might have been the best thing that happened to this group of upper-middle class, comfortably liberal, well-educated, mostly white suburbanites. The bonus: a fresh batch of newcomers, many of them young families, have come to join them in that mission.

"I once heard someone talking about this large church with a lot of gays," said Shelley Parnes, a mother of small children who left the Roman Catholic fold to join St. Bartholomew's. "I said, 'Good, that's a sign that this is an open, welcoming community.' If they'll accept someone who's gay, then they'll accept others for any reason. That's the kind of church I want my children to grow up in." The neighbors might not be happy, and some members remain a bit edgy, but their mission is clear—and contagious.

The brothers and sisters at Church of the Apostles have fully internalized that lesson, as well. This church plant is truly "mission-shaped": it sounds, looks, feels, and operates like the Seattle neighborhood where it's planted. That means it is truly alternative: alt-music, alt-worship, alt-culture. But don't be fooled by the "alt" title. COTA may be part-art collective, part-party promoter, but it is *all* church. They are just working with a different definition.

"We keep re-reading the Bible to get insights about what Jesus did," Pastor Karen Ward said. "Here's what we know: he traveled with a small core, and they did life together. They slept in some meadows, encountered large groups. A few of those they met actually listened and followed. Half of them were men and half were women. They went around trying to live the kingdom life and trying to tell people about it. We're trying to use the same paradigm."

That approach has taken the Apostles into territory most mainline churches do not venture near. For instance, COTA adapted to its culture by providing multiple entry points. Besides worship, members have run a tea bar where they provided Benedictine hospitality with a cup of Darjeeling. Some people link through an artists' collective called "artwerks," a separate nonprofit that serves as one of COTA's alter egos. Others connect through The Fremont Abbey, home for worship and a venue where musicians and artists of all ages book shows and support others' work.

And at the center of it all are the Apostles, that smaller band of brothers and sisters who are living "the kingdom life."

Curate Ryan Marsh and Mistress of Music Lacey Brown are part of that group. They live with four other friends in a house called Rosewood Manor. Together, they are shaping their own intentional Christian community, complete with a rule of life and daily prayer. Ward is the abbess to this countercultural band of "urban monks."

"I'm all about being poor and being with people," said Brown, a twenty-something who grew up in the Reformed tradition. "So much in our culture forces us to be alone." Marsh shared her concern. "Everybody is scattered from where they were raised," he said. "People never leave the house, never leave the computer. They scoff at the idea of family and community."

These young people are fierce about reclaiming community and connection, and they are passionate about sharing it in ways that speak to their context. "I'm just being myself and hoping others will be themselves, discover their gifts," Brown said. "I'm hoping to find God in my community and that my community finds God." That mission drives the Apostles into the world and brings the world right into their funky little abbey.

Identity

What Is It? The demographic markers like the church's size, median income, its dominant age, ethnicity, sexual orientation, ideology, etc.; also includes the defining culture and story of the community's life to this point.

The Signs: 1. The congregation values its history, traditions and denominational heritage; it also fosters an identity flexible enough to include The Other.

2. Leaders have consciously studied the make-up of the surrounding community and intentionally invited those neighbors to join and help to shape their common life and common mission.

3. The congregation is developing critical consciousness of who is inside, who is marginalized and who is outside, and why, and seeks to eliminate exclusionary barriers blocking The Other.

Seminary professor and South Indian church leader Christopher Duraisingh describes beautifully what happens when we open the bounds of our identity to embrace the myriad voices of fellow pilgrims around us:

> The story of God's love in Jesus Christ is like the bud of a fragrant flower, fully ripe but as yet only in the process of opening fully. As we read and hear the [gospel] from the variety of our languages and perspectives, multivoicedly, to use my phrase, each interpretation opens one petal of the gospel-flower. As each petal of the flower opens, we come to behold the loveliness of the blossoming flower and smell its fragrance . . . Only through a process of a multicultural, or multivoiced, opening up shall we discern that love in all its fullness.[4]

As Duraisingh intuits, the more we welcome new perspectives and voices fully into our lives, the bigger and fuller our knowledge of the world and of God, *and* the richer our identity as the body of Christ. Radically welcoming communities are in the business of saying yes to that opening, even if it means a de-centering, identity-shifting encounter with The Other.

At St. Mary's in West Harlem, the community has claimed a truly welcoming and flexible identity. Here, you meet Charles Kelly, a homeless man with matted hair and spry eyes who shows up in the robing room, dons his

---

4. Christopher Durasingh, "Toward a Postcolonial Re-Visioning," in Beyond Colonial Anglicanism: The Anglican Communion in the 21st Century, ed. Ian Douglas and Kwok Pui Lan (New York: Church Publishing Inc., 2001), 351.

alb and processes down the center aisle with confidence. And when he stands at the center of the
assembly to read Jesus' words, he is glowing, trans-
figured. "I was unemployed and I needed something
to eat, so I came to the Soup Kitchen," Kelly told
me. "It was different here. I felt these good vibes
and lots of love. It's like when I arrived, they asked
me, 'You want to cut the bread, help to make some
sandwiches? You want a job as a clean-up aide?'
They invited me to become part of it all."

> We believe the Holy Spirit
> embraces, protects, and cares
> for persons of every race, culture,
> gender, age, sexual orientation,
> economic circumstance, and be-
> lief. Holy Faith respects all people
> and we welcome everyone
> to worship with us.
>
> HOLY FAITH WELCOME STATEMENT

Here, middle-class Harlemites and Columbia
University professionals clap and praise alongside
those who first entered the church through the Soup Kitchen downstairs.
And for a time, in this place, they stand together. "Whoever you are—rich,
poor, from the streets, black, white, gay or straight—we are not afraid,"
parishioner Glenda Marie White told me as she pointed with pride to their
infamous "The 'I Am Not Afraid' Church" banner. "If you're here," she said,
"you're already one of us."

The community admittedly has a long history of pushing aside social
barriers and standing with the least of these. In the 1800s, they were the
first parish in the Diocese of New York (some say the country) to ban pew
rents. In the 1980s, they opened a shelter and later a hospice for victims of
the AIDS epidemic ravaging New York's gay community. Today, they are
working to stay aware of class stratification and discerning how to genuinely,
intentionally welcome gay and lesbian people.

With every new challenge, every new group that appears, the people of St.
Mary's have to say "yes" again to a Christian identity that is risky and runs coun-
ter to the larger Episcopal Church's culture. Nobody ever said it would feel
good. Middle-class members like Gloria Smith long for a more dignified service (with some concern, she said the choir rehearsals "sound like they're getting ready to go to a dance!"). But she continues to serve as the junior warden,
and she told me she is devoted to the community vision. "I went to another
black church in Harlem when their priest was installed. I put on my Sunday
best and walked in. Well, there was a big difference between the people inside
and who's outside in the neighborhood. It made me feel strange. I need to be
in a place where everybody's totally accepted." She found it at St. Mary's.

All Saints in Pasadena started from a radically different position. It's one
of the largest Episcopal congregations in the country, and yet, despite all their
power and experience, they couldn't seem to cross one barrier: the race divide.

Former rector George Regas led the congregation from the turbulent
1960s and into the social upheavals of the 1990s; he admitted to me that

he never poured the energy into dismantling racial oppression and analyzing white privilege that he did into other struggles. "I had zero experience with homosexuality when I came," he said, but members soon pushed him to new awareness. That never happened around race. "To get deeply into where you are [regarding race], how you became that, what you get out of it . . . we've had a hard time with that."

Race in Pasadena was simply a tough and nasty issue, especially for All Saints. In the 1940s they planted St. Barnabas, a separate congregation for their black servants. Since then, most All Saints members have assumed black people would prefer St. Barnabas. With so many layers and such deep-seated antagonism and mistrust, Regas said he never had the opportunity—or the will—to step into the quagmire of racism.

Christina Honchell works at the intersection between the surrounding community and the church. She pointed out yet another layer of privilege All Saints has yet to reckon with: economic privilege. "Honestly, I believe it all comes down to class. We're good at welcoming Latinos who are professionals and don't like noisy children. But poor people? I don't think even working-class whites would fit in here."

Given that tough reality, Honchell sees only one way out. It begins with engaging the community, listening to the people on the ground, getting to know the local public schools and workers, and building real relationships rather than trying to "do for." Then it takes bringing diverse cultures together in the sanctuary. "To be welcoming," she said, "you have to get people to really bump into each other, to pray and play with people they wouldn't see at work or at home."

Current rector Ed Bacon said he understands all that. But even bumping into each other takes work. It requires taking a hard look at your identity through both the race and class lenses. "We're perceived as a rich white folks' church. To change that, we've got to have meaningful relations with people of different races and classes. It's going to take getting the dominant, privileged class skilled enough to know their power and what happens when they walk into a room."

In the last decade, Bacon, the senior staff, committee heads, and other leaders and members have undergone anti-oppression trainings designed to give them a common language and conceptual foundation, along with an opportunity to identify systems of privilege in a structured, mediated environment. In true All Saints' style, they also crafted and widely disseminated a detailed plan for opening their doors and expanding their identity.[5] Year after year, they've increased their cultural competence and

---

5. Check out the plan on their website: www.allsaintspasadena.org.

broadened their commitment. And while they haven't arrived, they're finally positioned to launch a Spanish-language service as a base for ministry with area Latinos.

Knowing who you want to become and establishing a sense of urgency about moving from the current identity to one that embraces The Other—this, in itself, is a significant mark on the road to radical welcome.

Ministries and Relationships

What Is It?   Any practices of the congregation related to fulfilling the mission and dream: pastoral care, evangelism, community service, justice ministries, community life, stewardship, Christian formation, and external relationships.

The Signs   1. The congregation's activities have been thoughtfully organized to reflect and fulfill the radically welcoming mission.

2. Community ministries reflect mutuality and a desire for empowerment and transformation of self, other and community (doing *with* others, rather than doing *for* others).

3. Ministries draw members at the community's center and its margins into mutual, transforming relationship.

Radically welcoming churches are intentional about realigning their activities and relationships for mission. After all, where else do we practice radical welcome except on the ground, in ministries and community relationships that train us to be active participants in the constantly in-breaking reign of God? This is where we first encounter The Other and discover a common bond in our shared commitment to the dream of God.

Kenneth Adams, a black native of Los Angeles, saw it work that way at Holy Faith in Inglewood, California. When black people began to arrive some thirty years ago, the welcome was far from warm. The parish history cites a particularly painful incident from that early chapter. One of the first black parishioners had volunteered in the church office and was busy opening the mail. He found a response to the parish survey, which asked how best to improve Holy Faith. The respondent simply wrote, "Get rid of the niggers."

Adams arrived during that dicey period. "When I came here, the church was 99 percent white. It was rather strange. Several whites were bending over backward to welcome us. Some whites left." Over time he said the members who remained formed relationships across boundaries, creating and then serving together in a variety of ministries and small groups. Veteran members like Adams, along with his dedicated white counterparts, set an example as the bridge-builders, literally paving the way for more and more people from both communities to meet and build a common life in Christ.

Former rector Gary Commins shepherded the community through more recent changes with the same intentionality. "We had programs and conversations and asked: What do you really treasure in your culture? And then we asked, How does your culture express prejudice?" Eventually, they formed a task force, created a curriculum and shared it with other churches working through issues of cultural diversity and inclusion. They made the commitment and then concretized it as part of their formation and community ministries. They equipped themselves for change.

> This family system has always been hospitable in a noblesse oblige way. It was not okay to be rude. That's tacky. And for years, their money kept the diocesan Indian programs going. That's the history: bearing the white man's burden. The real stuff happens at the next stage, where there's real, one-to-one engagement.
>
> HOWARD ANDERSON, (FORMERLY) ST. PAUL'S-DULUTH

St. Paul's in Duluth, Minnesota, is living proof of the difference relationships make: these connections change neighborhoods; they can also change a church.

Over the years, St. Paul's had generously responded to community needs, but parishioners told me it was generally from a privileged, Lady Bountiful-like distance. So while they are proud of their work in the 1970s sponsoring and shepherding families fleeing Cambodia and Vietnam and supporting Indian ministries throughout the Diocese of Minnesota, members did not push beyond their comfort zone on a regular basis. And while some poor and non-white neighbors entered the church, they rarely stuck around for very long.

Architecture did not help the welcoming cause. Built in 1915, this venerable stone edifice looks like a fortress, and for too many years that is just what the neighbors thought it was. The hinge on the 300-pound doors was set so low you could barely open the doors. Visitors would never have known the doors were even unlocked. If that sounds like an apt metaphor, it is. "We knew the neighborhood was changing, but the congregation was still basically a small, insiders' parish financed and influenced by a small group of old men," said Elaine Killen, who has been at St. Paul's for nearly sixty years. "We needed people who could help us to open up, go out on a limb."

They called Howard Anderson, hoping he would do the job. "I told them if I came I'd want to change some things, but I guaranteed that I'd add 100 people in the first year." He was true to his word. Average Sunday attendance doubled in his ten-year tenure, jumping from 175 to 350 people. They list nearly 1,000 active members.

Anderson now leads the Cathedral College at Washington National Cathedral. During his years at St. Paul's, he led the community on a wild ride—always keeping the ministry of pastoral care at the forefront. A huge team of priests, deacons and trained lay leaders visit hospitals, nursing homes, homes, and any other place where people were lonely or hurting. "When you're doing this left-wing 'pinko' stuff, they need to know you love them," Anderson said. "Then they'll feel safe enough to go with you any-where. So we've gone slow, let people know we love them without patron-izing them. It's possible to gain young adults and reach out to the neighbor-hood and not lose your older, wealthier, more conservative members. Just don't pull the rug out from under anyone."

That doesn't mean they didn't take any risks. To launch their new com-mitment to the neighborhood, St. Paul's tithed 10 percent of the proceeds from their million-dollar capital campaign and invested it in neighborhood outreach. *Then* they invited neighborhood and civic leaders to join them in discerning how the resources could best be used. Suddenly, St. Paul's was no longer Lady Bountiful riding about town, dropping favors on the lowly. Now the congregation was entering genuine partnership, laying itself open to the needs of the community.

According to Duluth native Jackie Johnson, that was the moment when St. Paul's finally became a real neighbor. "This church had a reputation," said Johnson, who has observed the church from a distance most of her life. "The money people were the parishioners, and everything was geared to that group. We've come a long way. My mother-in-law was a housekeeper here for many years. Now look at it. They want us to come in."

One popular church-sponsored program, the Mind 2 Mind summer enrichment program, has drawn a whole new generation to the church build-ing. Kids who skirted the forbidding old church now think of it as their second home. When vandals tried to deface the church, one leader told me, a couple of kids ran in and stopped them, yelling, "You're not gonna touch my church!"

Besides Mind 2 Mind, St. Paul's hosts dozens of community groups and sponsors several of its own community ministries: a neighborhood center next door, the Little Treasures child care center, a parish nurse who serves the community, a computer lab in their carriage house, and more. The for-tress walls have come tumbling down.

With fewer walls in place, St. Paul's has been touched by its community relationships like never before. In the past, by virtue of their power, mem-bers could always choose to maintain critical distance from their beneficia-ries. Now parishioners have a chance to get involved and form new, mutually transforming relationships with their neighbors. "Let me tell you how much our comfort zones have shifted," said Terry Parsons, the church's Director of Lay Ministries. "People here used to say anyone on welfare must be a bad person. Now I go with people to pick up their food stamps. That's a change."

Someday St. Paul's may take those new relationships to the next level and welcome their neighbors to join the church's common life on the inside. Grace Episcopal Church in Lawrence, Massachusetts, didn't have to wait: the marginalized members had already come in. The two groups just had no idea how to relate with one another. It took common ministries to build real community—inside the church and outside.

That didn't come easily. A congregational development consultant met with Latino and Anglo leaders to figure out their future together, helping them to name their frustrations in a structured environment. Parishioners kept talking and discovered shared hopes. They found they wanted to model a different way of approaching change, for the sake of their parish, their neighborhood and the wider church. "There are a lot of us '8 a.m. saints' who don't want to bend," Carol St. Louis told me. "But if you don't bend, you might break. I've seen other churches close because they couldn't bend and accommodate new people. That's not going to be us."

The consultant told them they needed two things: better communication and shared ministries. So they branched out, drawing members from the English- and Spanish-speaking congregations together to offer computer skills and language courses to the neighborhood. They also hosted regular dinners and fellowship events for the express purpose of bringing the communities together and building friendship across the race and class divide.

Those intentional efforts have slowed over the years, but the seeds still bear life. Fran Kuchar sees it. A white woman who has been part of the Grace community for more than thirty years, she watches a steady stream of Latinos of all ages coming to the church for everything from worship to computer classes to women's prayer groups to neighborhood youth jams. Once, it might have disturbed her. Now she welcomes the challenge, because she sees where it is headed. "Sure, if we come together there will be things we lose. But look at all we gain: a place that's full of people and filled with so much spirit you can touch it."

Leadership and Feedback Systems

What Is It?   The set of mechanisms that enable a group to reflect effectively, make decisions, act, and other-wise exercise power

The Signs   1. Leaders are intentionally recruited, mentored and selected from the distinct groups in the community, with special attention to building power among the under-represented margins.

2. There is wide access to decision-makers and transparency regarding decision-making.

3. Different cultural and generational styles of leadership are understood and creatively accommodated.

People on the margins know the importance of power, mostly because institutional power is so often withheld from them. They know there can be no genuine, radical welcome without a sharing of power.

St. Philip's-Harlem has a mixed history when it comes to sharing power with The Other. They're strong on black liberation. But as one of New York's flagship black Episcopal churches, they also have their share of hang-ups about tradition, class and keeping up appearances, and thus who "ought" to be in leadership.

For a time, that worked perfectly for Sidney and Philip Blake-Spivey, a professional couple in their fifties. "I think we're both seen as the Good Negro and the Good Gay," Philip said. "We're professional, we're active, we're well-spoken, and people treat us like we're special. Maybe that makes us easier to take, but there is something we can do. We can raise sensitivity to class, ageism and sexuality. We can bring those up. They'll try to normalize us, but we'll keep on bringing those issues up again."

Cecily Broderick y Guerra partnered with leaders like the Blake-Spiveys to crank the system open for younger, less "acceptable" gay and lesbian leaders. "[Sidney and Philip] are among the most respected leaders in the congregation, partly because their social background and family constellation matched this stratified system," she explained. "We're capitalizing on that opening to get a group of younger gay leaders out there."

Broderick y Guerra said the strategy is working. She has groomed and mentored gay and lesbian newcomers and advocated for their appointment to task forces and subcommittees of the vestry, and she said it's making a difference. "The vestry agreed to pick several leaders to send to a diocesan training. Four of the twelve are from Epiphany (the black gay and lesbian group based at St. Philip's). Is that tokenism? It would be poor stewardship if we didn't capitalize on their leadership."

LGBT people come together at St. Philip's for Epiphany, a gathering of black Episcopalians (and others) who are "in the life." From that home base, several partnered lesbians and gay men have felt secure enough to step up as part of the church's core leadership. And several older members said

> I thought it was symbolic that of the six originally asked to be Journey to Adulthood and Rite 13 mentors, four were gay or lesbian. That's extremely important. It's one thing to put gay men on the Altar Guild. It's something else to put us teaching the kids.
>
> MAGGIE KULYK,
> ST. BARTHOLOMEW'S-ATLANTA

hosting Epiphany and having out people as leaders has actually given them something to brag about.

I met one of those church mothers, Beatrice Tomilson, who fairly preened as she informed me, "I've told my friends with lesbian kids that they need to come here. And the people who started Epiphany? They came here because of me. They visited one Sunday, and I called them and told them they should come back and join." Even as she spoke the words, she looked with a smile to her adopted granddaughter, Dorothy Carlton, a 19-year-old out lesbian who has led the church's young women's service guild.

Chuck Allen is one of the men Beatrice Tomlinson welcomed years ago. He appreciates her open arms. He also promises it will prove mutually beneficial. "Gay people are going to save St. Philip's and this entire diocese," he said. "We're going to teach them that they can be open enough to save themselves. All they have to do is practice welcome. God will do the rest." Allen and his lesbian and gay sisters and brothers are leading St. Philip's right into the dream of God.

At All Saints-Pasadena, black and Latino members told me their struggle to obtain power is a daily one. "I think a lot of people thought, because I'm Latino, I would bring in the Latinos," said Abel Lopez, an Anglican from Cuba who serves on the All Saints clergy staff. "I said, 'No, I'm not going to do anything to get Latinos or blacks or anybody else until this environment changes.' This community has to learn how to do power-sharing. I want us to be inclusive, but we have to do it the right way, and we're not there yet."

Associate rector Wilma Jakobsen came to All Saints from South Africa. A white woman who worked closely with Archbishop Desmond Tutu, she said she was shocked by how few people of color she saw when she first visited the church—especially in positions of power. "This community went ten years with no priest of color. My antenna goes up when I hear that. Something's going on, and it's an issue for people who love justice to pay attention to."

She took the job because she saw a real desire to change and to deal with root causes and questions of power. "One of the reasons I wanted to come here was because of the intentionality," she said. "I saw the commitment to looking at power dynamics. I saw people in little positions saying things to people in big positions."

Thanks to the work of leaders like Jakobsen and Lopez—and rector Ed Bacon's willingness to use his own power to open doors for others—there's been real change. The rota of readers and lay ministers always includes people of color, and they've hired and nurtured a number of clergy of color. Some white members have complained that Bacon is engaged in crass tokenism, and they resent the fact that there are not as many slots open to them. Bacon told me he sees the bigger picture and hopes others will, too. "The Eucharistic table should look more like L.A. and more like heaven," he said. "I know that's a 'diversity' move and not multiculturalism, but it's a slow process, and we started here."

Over time, the entire congregational leadership system is also being transformed from the inside out. Those who want to take part in high-profile ministries and overseas missions are required to participate in Visions, an anti-oppression, consciousness-raising program based in Arlington, Massachusetts.[6] It's made a difference. "The clergy and committee chairs and lots more leaders are getting the training, and that is informing our work," Lopez told me. "I have to ask, What does leadership mean to me as a young man of color in a meeting with all women? This is where the real tension is, for all of us."

It may be a tense position to stake out, but All Saints' leaders are realizing that no power equals no welcome.

At Grace Church in Lawrence, the congregation's efforts to make change and become welcoming stalled until they finally learned to talk about power. There were two worship gatherings: a dwindling white service and a thriving Latino one. With each day, the tension and resentment started to build. The relationship between the two was essentially Anglo landlord–Latino tenant. No one wanted to touch the elephant in the room: the white parishioners' fear of handing over the reins to Latinos with different cultural values, a different ecclesiology and different leadership styles. "The old guard was willing to let [Latino] people be members, but not to be the leaders," said Ennis Duffis, the priest-in-charge.

Their first foray into shared power came when white and Latino members collaborated on common ministries to serve the city of Lawrence. Eventually, the old guard agreed to form mentoring relationships with the newer, Latino members and experimented with surrendering more control.

The key was people like Migdalia Mendez, who stepped up and created links between the new leaders and the older ones. "I've been called the bridge," she said. "I came to Grace fifteen years ago and was one of the few who stayed. In some way, I felt I belonged. People asked me to be part of things. In the Catholic Church, no one asked me to be this involved." Now, Mendez and other key leaders take responsibility for helping others to stay the course for real transformation.

They've also listened and helped their community to hold the fear of change. Through intentional feedback sessions, members could share their concerns *and* passions. Latino members like Elsa Berroa could voice their

---

6. For more information on Visions, please consult the bibliography.

lack of excitement about traditional Anglo liturgy and decorum. "Some people think there's only one way to do church," she said. "They squeeze the
children if they make noise, because church is supposed to be quiet. Well,
I think that's just boring." Berroa and other Latino leaders also shared their
frustration at being shut out of leadership because of white perceptions of
what it takes to hold authority. Meanwhile, senior white members like Pauline Messer, who has called the church home for fifty years, could admit that
they found the Spanish-speaking service too large (about 200 on an average
Sunday) and too loud (with a praise band and children present for the entire
service.) It was freeing for everyone to finally tell the truth.

There is still some tug-of-war, but now the vestry more closely resem-
bles the congregation: Mendez, the Latina senior warden, heads a council
that includes eight Latinos and three whites. And people know they don't
have to whisper in corners or feel like tenants. It may be less than "proper,"
but it's everyone's home now.

Worship

What Is It?   The complex of ritual activities that serve to gather God's
people and foster relationship with God and with each other
through prayer, praise, sacrament, and Scripture[7]

The Signs   1. The make-up of the worshiping body—which may be
spread over more than one service—reflects the surrounding
community.

2. Liturgical texts, music, images, and worship leaders reflect
the congregation and surrounding community.

3. The community's worship is lively and reflective, deeply
rooted in lived traditions, yet open to fresh expressions (again,
not necessarily in a single service).

There's no one way to reflect radical welcome in the context of worship. For
instance, Howard Anderson told me he was dying to have more fun with
the liturgy at St. Paul's in Duluth. ("I get bored by it," he confessed.) But
he knew members needed an anchor, and it was liturgy. So they kept the
formal, spoken Rite I Eucharist at 8 a.m., and priests only stopped facing
the back wall a few years ago. "People need a home base," Anderson said,
"then they can venture out."

---

7. Adapted from "What is corporate worship?" in the Cathechism, Book of Common
Prayer, 857.

Holy Faith-Inglewood has committed to performing that delicate balancing act and still embracing the gifts of whites, African Americans, Africans, Latinos, and women. On any given Sunday, you can start the morning at a conventional Anglican service with music from the standard hymnal and an inclusivized Book of Common Prayer liturgy. Stay in your seat and you will witness a longer, even more inclusive BCP liturgy, featuring music from the church's homemade hymnbook, which boasts selections from the many cultures that call Holy Faith home. Depending on the Sunday, you may also get to fall in behind Nigerian members who lead the rest of the congregation (including some awkward but enthusiastic white members) in a dancing, singing offertory procession to the altar. You can then finish the afternoon with a folksy Spanish-language service for families and children that features guitars, maracas and songbooks with no musical notation at all (which makes the hymns accessible to those who don't read music).

And several times a year, all those groups come together for a family reunion-style bilingual service, something their bilingual rector, Altagracia Perez, delights in leading.

Holy Faith has crafted a body of liturgies that speak to their cultural context, uphold the essentials of the tradition, and express their shared faith and hope in Christ. It can feel a bit of a hodge-podge, but Nigerian lay leader and cradle Anglican Daniel Mogbo told me he never doubts that they are firmly in the Anglican tradition, even if they are sometimes outside of convention. "There are essentials of Christianity that you don't compromise. Then there are the nonessentials that are subject to cultural norms and conditions. Jesus is God. No argument on that. How do we sing? Use a hymnal? Sing five praise songs? Stand up? Sit down? Dance while processing? These are decisions each group has to make. There's nothing Anglican or Episcopalian about those choices." If anything, the quintessentially Anglican response is one that honors its context as well as it does the tradition.

The crew at Church of the Apostles in Seattle could not agree more. They gather for a weekly Eucharist, but not on Sunday mornings. Honoring their context, their main worship gathering is on Saturdays at 5 p.m. in The Fremont Abbey, the converted church building that serves as the community's art gallery, music venue and sanctuary.

When it's time to worship, the service follows the same basic structure—the *ordo*, for Latin lovers—that Christians have been following for millennia: gathering, word, meal, sending. But the Apostles weave in art and film

> There have definitely been some protests about what Ed is doing with the altar (holding spots open for LEMs of color). You hear a lot of, "This is tokenism. I used to be a LEM and now, because of these 'other folks,' I can't."
>
> STEPHEN CHENEY-RICE,
> ALL SAINTS-PASADENA

on video screens; electronic, ambient music by their house band; meditation and group reflection with the Scripture appointed for the day; original prayers for confession and forgiveness; icons created by young artists in the community; and a variety of entry points and worship foci that recall the energy and movement of Orthodox liturgies. From week to week, they crack open The Word in creative, stirring ways, but they're always grounded in The Word. The resulting blend is a unique and surprisingly Anglican amalgam of ancient and future, catholic (that is, connected to the church universal) and reformed (that is, connected to its cultural location).

To Ryan Marsh, a media arts wiz and gifted musician, that kind of translation and adaptation is what worship is all about. "If you look around, you'll see that the Church has been doing this—taking from one part of the culture and applying it to the Church—forever. So how does that happen in our culture? Maybe you play Björk instead of Bach. At some point, you've got to not be afraid of things in the culture that are usually separate. If there's a DJ spinning trance, then maybe there's a spiritual element that you couldn't see in the original context. We want to bring that out." If liturgy is the work of the people—drawn from the Greek *laos* (people) and *ergon* (work)—then the people at COTA are definitely doing their work.

GO DEEPER . . .

1. Which of the stories, comments or ideas you just read was the most challenging? Exciting? How do they connect with your own story? What do they inspire you to ask or to do?

2. How do these reflections link with your church's story, or the stories of churches you've known?

3. Look again at the signs of radical welcome associated with each part of congregational life. Have you seen churches or other communities that show these signs? What was it like to be in such a community? Did they welcome in some areas and not in others? Did they welcome some groups and not others? What was the story behind their willingness to welcome?

4. Have you seen communities that do not demonstrate signs of radical welcome? What was it like to be in such a community? Did they welcome in some areas and not in others? Did they welcome some groups and not others? What was the story behind their lack of welcome?

PART III

The Practice of Radical Welcome

Re-imagine Your Common Life

The call to ministry is the call to be a citizen of the kingdom
of God in a new way, the daring, free, accepting,
compassionate way Jesus modeled. It means being bound
by no yesterday, fearing no tomorrow, drawing no lines
between friend and foe, the acceptable ones and the outcasts.
Ministry is commitment to the dream of God.

VERNA DOZIER, *THE DREAM OF GOD*[1]

W e all can and should take individual responsibility for living radical
welcome. The revolution means nothing if it doesn't result in new
hearts, new behaviors, new convictions. Alas, most of us would probably
prefer to limit radical welcome—or any transformation—to the personal
and interpersonal level. But radical welcome has to go deeper, into the very
marrow of your congregational life. A community cannot hope to live faithfully and fully as the body of Christ without re-imagining its structures in
order to make room for The Other. You can refresh the wine you pour. You
must also fashion new wineskins.

In what ways can you re-imagine and reconfigure your common life to
fulfill the radically welcoming dream of God? You could consult a number
of change process manuals.[2] But if you wish to consider not only how to

---

1. Dozier, 139.

2. I have found Gil Rendle and Alice Mann's *Holy Conversations: Strategic Planning as a
Spiritual Practice for Congregations*, Jim Herrington et al., *Leading Congregational Change:*

Online Extra: Exercises for Discerning the Dream of God in Your Community

change but what to change, you'll need some extra tools. In this chapter, you will have the chance to turn your gaze inward, assessing how your congregation's bodylife can reflect and further God's dream in your context.[3]

Look at the five broad areas and start to imagine where change needs to happen in your community, if The Other on the margins of your community's life is to find a warm, hospitable space and a welcome table.

Mission and Vision

Why revisit and possibly reconfigure your mission? Bluntly stated, too many mainline Christians have made a deal with our churches: provide us with security, stability, control, beauty, comfort, familiarity, pain alleviation, intimacy, and family. Be our home and refuge. In exchange, we will attend worship faithfully, contribute our money and various talents, join in service to those in need, and offer devotion to Christ. For many, the deal is off if the church pushes or challenges us to live into values that compromise our current way of life. We balk if we sense the ground shifting under us. Most of us want to live and love well. We did not come here for radical transformation.

> The church's mission is no longer about us; now it is about God, whose mission is sure to conflict with some of our own most heartfelt desires.

Say "yes" to Jesus, and you have agreed to rewrite the terms of the contract. You begin to live as if "[i]t's not the church of God that has a mission, but the God of mission who has a church."[4] The church's mission is no longer about us; now it is about God, whose mission is sure to conflict with some of our own most heartfelt desires. We are more than our buildings, more than our liturgies. We are more than a family, more than an intimate, friendly group that shares certain culturally or historically rooted practices. We are God's partners in loving a new world into being. The question is, how can you serve and partner with God in this radical adventure, given your context?

A Practical Guide for the Transformational Journey, Gil Rendle's *Leading Change in the Congregation: Spiritual and Organizational Tools for Leaders*, and Eric Law's *Sacred Acts, Holy Change* to be clear, effective, systematic guides to designing and implementing planned change processes.

3. Adapted from Herrington et al., Leading Congregational Change, 149–51.

4. Tim Dearborn, quoted in Archbishop's Council, Mission-Shaped Church: Church Planting and Fresh Expressions of Church in a Changing Context (London: Church House Publishing, 2004), 85.

Elements of Your Congregational Bodylife	Main Guiding Questions for Discernment
Mission and Vision	How could your stated purpose and plans for the future reflect the dream of God?
Identity	Who does the dream of God call you to include as fully present and empowered members of your congregation?
Ministries and Relationships	What kinds of activities and relationships reflect the radically welcoming dream of God? How could your ministries and relations more fully proclaim, fulfill and prepare you for that dream?
Leadership and Feedback Systems	How is God calling you to recast leadership and to expand your notion of who is truly worthy of exercising power? How could you create structures for feedback that allow more voices to be heard and honored?
Worship	How could your liturgy and music reflect the dream of God for your community? What would it communicate about your community's culture(s), values and mission?

Your mission statement is where you get to define the clear, shared and compelling description of God's purpose for your congregation.[5] You may also drop to the next level, from the long-term mission to the more specific vision, a detailed yet concise and compelling picture of the preferred future to which you believe God is calling your congregation in the next three to five years.[6] There are resources aplenty for designing your mission and vision statements, including the ever-useful *Studying Congregations Handbook*[7] and *Holy Conversations*. In "Bread for the Journey," part of the online companion to this book, you will find exercises designed to guide congregations in finding specific language and images to name their own dream of radical welcome.

Whatever language and content you arrive at—and even if you opt not to write a mission statement but to determine and communicate your values and purpose in other ways—some sense of commonly discerned and agreed upon direction is crucial. At a minimum, consider how you would complete the following statements:

5. Herrington et al., *Leading Congregational Change*, 49.

6. Ibid.

7. Nancy Ammerman, Jackson Carroll, Carl Dudley, and William McKinney, editors. See bibliography for full details.

> Through the Church, God is acting to . . .
> In this church, we are joining God by . . .

The text and/or images you use to fill in those blanks will set you on the path to discerning the overall mission of the church of God (the first query) and how your particular congregation lives into it (the second).

Once you've got your mission and vision, don't be afraid to proclaim them and to use them to hold yourselves accountable. Think of St. Mary's-West Harlem's banner: "The 'I Am Not Afraid' Church!" Whenever they walk by it, members have to think about whether they're fulfilling that mission today. Or consider this statement from All Saints-Pasadena:

> In grateful response to the love of God made tangible in Jesus Christ, the faith community of All Saints Church is called
>
> - to embody God's unlimited and inclusive love that embraces, liberates and empowers people, whoever they are and wherever they find themselves on their journey of faith
>
> - to live out Christ's vision of unlimited love that empowers new life not only for children, youth and adults within our membership but with other neighbors, especially those who suffer from violence, injustice and bigotry.

The statement is simple, clear, comprehensive. It distills well: their website opens to an image and the words, "Whoever you are and wherever you find yourself on your journey of faith, you are welcome here." Best of all, it's more than talk; you can look at their internal and external ministries, including aggressive efforts to increase the presence and power of marginalized people, and see how it flows from the mission.

Transforming Your Mission and Vision

Take another look at the "Mission and Vision" signs and stories in part 2 (pp. 77–80). Then carefully consider these questions:

Where Are We Now?

- What is your church's mission or vision? Is it publicly stated? Did the congregation have any input?
- What does it communicate about what you value and how you practice your values?
- Does the mission/vision actually shape what you do and how you look as a community? Does it get preached? Do committees and leaders reference it as they develop programs?

- What is already radically welcoming about your mission and vision? How can this positive experience equip you for the work ahead?

Where Is God Inviting Us to Go?

- How could you reconfigure your mission or vision so that it reflects your commitment to radical welcome? How could you invite the community to take part in that visioning process?

- In what ways can you ensure that the fresh mission or vision affects the church's decisions and direction?

- How could you make sure you hold yourselves accountable to this vision of God's dream for you?

Identity

How you define your community's identity, particularly whom you include and embrace, communicates volumes about you. If you seek to live into the dream of God, you should be even more intentional about drawing the boundaries of your community. Imagine Jesus' table fellowship and community of outcasts. Then try stretching the limits of your own circle to embrace The Other.

But who is The Other, the stranger, the one on the margins of *your* community whom God calls you to embrace and be changed by? This is certainly a question of power relations and context. The black, straight, middle-class church in Harlem filled with mostly seniors may need to pay attention to the gay men and lesbians, Latinos and Asians, poor people, and young adults who have flooded the neighborhood but remained at the church's margins. The predominantly white church in a multicultural urban or suburban context should open its eyes and doors to the incredible economic, generational, sexual, and racial diversity at its doorstep. Wherever you are placed, you have the chance to examine how you reflect the cultural, socioeconomic and generational diversity of your surroundings. More than that, you have the chance to extend the bounds of your own identity and to engage in Christlike embrace of The Other.

> Wherever you are placed, you have the chance to examine how you reflect the cultural, socioeconomic and generational diversity of your surroundings. More than that, you have the chance to extend the bounds of your own identity and to engage in Christlike embrace of The Other.

When it's time to get concrete about who is nearby but not radcially welcomed, a variety of resources can help congregations to identify and analyze the demographic make-up of their neighborhood, region or diocese.[8] But there's nothing like getting out, on foot, and walking the environs. Try talking to civic leaders who've had to make it their business to know the neighborhood, who is in it, and how it is changing.

That on-the-ground assessment pairs well with another one: The Pew Review. Jane Oasin, the Social Justice Ministries Officer at the Episcopal Church Center, suggests this exercise for congregations, and it's a simple one. Look at the people in the pews and then look at the ones on the sidewalk. "If they don't look the same," she warned, "then your church is going to stagnate or die." And lest anyone think only white churches should worry, she added, "This is true of churches of every race. I know a black Episcopal church in New Jersey; it's in the fifth poorest area in the country, but there are no poor people in the church. It doesn't reflect the neighborhood. Almost all the members have driven in. If anyone there wants to expand, they're going to have to reach out. Otherwise, they will die."

The drive to survive motivates lots of communities. According to Gregory Jacobs, many churches are fixated on "the Three M's: Mission, Money, and Maintenance" and how new people can help them with those priorities. Still others hope to become "diverse." I call this the acquisition model, as in, "We'd like to have more of them." None of these motivations will take you far. "If you're doing this because you want 'those people' to be with you, then that's paternalistic, materialistic, and condescending," Oasin told me. Echoing Paul's challenge to the Corinthians, she continued, "This is entirely about being whole, as God made us whole. If you're operating as a part, it's like being a body without one leg. You can't know the mind of God, be the body of Christ, if you don't represent or at least have relationship with the whole spectrum. If you view it as a task, a burden, and not as an opportunity and a gift, then you won't do it." Only the dream of God can compel you to seek this level of wholeness as a body.

Some will try to tell you embracing fresh voices in this way will jeopardize your core identity and threaten your ability to attract new members. They're only partly right. If you mumble a lukewarm, hesitant, bland welcome that says, "We're okay with everything because we don't really care about anything," no one is inspired by that! It's something else entirely to proclaim your radically welcoming identity with clarity and gospel integrity. Imagine the power of announcing, as Glenda Marie White at St. Mary's-West Harlem does, that, "If you are here, you are already one of us." If you

---

8. It's not a cure-all, but a starter resource is The Census: httpsilldata.census.gov/cedsci. Go deeper with Mission Insite, Mapdash, or the Study Your Congregation resource at: www.generalconvention.org.

have felt the pain and loss of being separated from another part of the body of Christ, and you want to heal the rift, then say so. Proclaim your conviction even as you continue to hold and be shaped by the culture, history, values, commitments, and even many of the preferences that have made you who you are. Have faith and leap with Christ, trusting that many yearning souls will be drawn and compelled by this invitation not just to attend your church but to share your life.

Transforming Your Identity

Take another look at the "Identity" signs and stories in part 2 (pp. 80–83). Then carefully consider these questions:

Where Are We Now?

- Who are you? Take stock of the congregation's dominant races, ethnicities, linguistic groups, ages, sexual orientations, class backgrounds, regional affiliations, physical abilities, and so forth.
- Which cultural, racial, age, economic groups values have historically shaped your congregation and its practices? How?
- Which groups shape the congregation and its practices—who are the "insiders"—today? What is the story behind this pattern?
- Which groups have historically been on the church's margins, either inside or just outside? Why?
- Which groups are inside the congregation but disempowered today? What is the story behind this pattern?
- Which groups of people live within a one-mile radius? Are they part of the congregation? If so, why? If not, what is the story behind this pattern?
- What is already radically welcoming about your identity? How does this prepare you for the work ahead?

Where Is God Inviting Us to Go?

- Who is The Other on the margins of your community?
- How could you publicly, authentically proclaim your desire to radically welcome, particularly with groups usually left on the margins?
- How could you prepare members for embracing the culture and identity of people coming from the margins?

Ministries and Relationships

What is ministry? Remember theologian Verna Dozier's words: "Ministry is commitment to the dream of God."[9] Given that calling, you can boldly ask, "What activities can we engage in to make the world more as God would have it be? What activities prepare us to be active participants in the constantly in-breaking reign of God?"

The possibilities are endless, mostly because churches are already engaged in a vast array of ministries and relationships within and beyond the parish walls. So start with what you have on the ground. Look at the existing ministries, and then imagine whether and how each ministry could even more fully engage and proclaim your common mission. It's worth being intentional. Ministries are the most obvious—and often the least threatening—place where lives connect and change.

> Go to your neighborhood ministry partners and listen to the actual needs of the community, and listen carefully to their answers, rather than go in with your own priorities and invite The Other to come on board.

According to the Right Reverend Arthur Williams, congregations with few members from the margins should really focus on ministries and relationships. "In some cases, a congregation can begin by responding around justice issues and social service needs in the community," said Williams, the Episcopal Church Center's Director of Ethnic Congregational Development. "That brings them into contact with others. Of course, the concern then is getting into the paternalistic, Lady Bountiful mode. Still, this moves people into their communities. And as they work together on justice issues, the relationships come up around it." To avoid the tendency toward paternalism, follow the St. Paul's-Duluth model: go to your neighborhood ministry partners and ask about the actual needs of the community, and listen carefully to their answers, rather than go in with your own priorities and invite The Other to come on board. You might also get involved with grassroots, broad-based community organizations, including those affiliated with the Industrial Areas Foundation, Gamaleil Foundation, or Pacific Institute for Community Organization.[10] Time and again, I've seen these groups broker relationships between disparate communities. Are you located in the suburbs or a small town? Most of these broad-based organizations encompass wide areas and connect people

---

9. Dozier, *The Dream of God*, 139.

10. Groups like the Industrial Areas Foundation, the Gamaleil Foundation and the Pacific Institute for Community Organization (PICO) serve as umbrella organizations that plant and nurture faith-based, broad-based community organizations across the United States and beyond. For more information, see the bibliography.

across geographic, racial, class, linguistic, generational, and denominational backgrounds.

This may be the best way to build new connections to different communities, even those with whom the church has had a contentious relationship. In the process, you will increase your own competence as a community that knows how to interact mutually and lovingly with people who have been marginalized and disempowered. Finally, valuable as they are in their own right, these deepened connections could also pave the way for welcoming neighbors and marginalized people to become part of the full life of the congregation.

Transforming Your Ministries and Relationships

Take another look at the "Ministries and Relationships" signs and stories in part 2 (pp. 84–88). Then carefully consider these questions:

Where Are We Now?

- What ministries are you engaged in? Take account of pastoral care, evangelism, community service, justice ministries, community life, stewardship, Christian formation, and external relationships.
- What are the stated ministry goals? What are the implicit ministry goals?
- Which groups tend to participate in which ministries? Are there some conspicuous patterns: groups who only work with each other, ministries that remain segregated along some demographic line? Why are these patterns present?
- In your social ministries, who is serving and who is being served; in other words, are you "doing for" The Other or "doing with"?
- Who are your ministry partners? How do you relate to your ministry partners; in other words, who holds the power to control your external partnerships?
- What is already radically welcoming about your ministries and relationships? How will this prepare you for the work ahead?

Where Is God Inviting Us to Go?

- What activities and relationships would most fully reflect and prepare you to live into your mission? Are there new ministries that would reflect your mission and your hope for radical welcome?
- How could your current ministries help people to build authentic, mutual relationships between members and with your neighbors?

- How could your ministries and relationships empower people, transform systems, and enable others to find their voices and speak their truths?
- More specifically, how could you engage in . . .

  — care-giving that serves both pastorally (helping people to heal and reckon with hurt) and prophetically (challenging people to test and stretch into vulnerable areas)?

  — evangelism that more effectively reaches marginalized people where they are and on their own terms?

  — community engagement that looks less like serving "them" and more like genuine partnership?

  — becoming an ally with those who lack your power and access, advocating and seeking justice in the wider community and society?

  — community gatherings and celebrations that reflect the priorities and styles of different groups?

  — formation programs and other activities that help members and/or ministry partners to share stories and cross boundaries?

  — stewardship programs that truly welcome the gifts of all members, sincerely highlighting the value of time and talent and not just large financial contributions?

Leadership and Feedback Systems

When you begin to imagine your leadership and feedback systems anew, you're touching a very tender spot: Who will be at the decision-making table? Who should have access to the clergy and leaders? What sort of clergy might we hire? Whose voice will be heard and honored? There is no way here to avoid the discussion of power, and church folk are among the most hesitant to raise that topic. Doesn't Jesus call us to surrender power? Then why should anyone seek it? Why on earth are we talking about it?

Offer the mentoring and encouragement—and, if necessary, reconfigure your own leadership structures—to make new leaders feel truly, radically welcomed.

Genuine, mutual relationship simply is not possible if one dominant group (or a cadre of groups) continues to order life for the whole. People who have stood at the margins know this, and so we often wait for the signal that power could shift before joining institutions run by a privileged group. The real proof of welcome is whether partners share their common life, including the power to order it.

Why is it so difficult to open and share power? Probably because it requires more than inviting a few token representatives to serve on committees (although, frankly, that may be a starting place). Ultimately, it requires us to surrender control, grow to trust each other, and even shift our expectations and definitions of "good" leadership. Systems of oppression make that tough to do. Certain groups have been depicted as less competent, less prepared, less trustworthy, and generally less equipped to exercise power. As a result, the empowered insiders consciously and subconsciously struggle with the fear that these marginalized members can't be trusted with leadership. Fitness to hold power has always depended on passing the "resume test" or exuding a culturally specific air of authority, and as Thom Chu has noticed, that ensures certain groups will never stand on equal footing. "If you want to be a deputy to General Convention or even a delegate to Diocesan Convention, there's a long resume barrier," said Chu, the Program Director for the Ministries with Young People Cluster at the Episcopal Church Center. "If you're younger, you simply can't have the same resume a Baby Boomer has. That's emblematic of how we say we want something but it doesn't come out on the other end."

For many of the same reasons, people moving from the margins to the center may have a difficult time finally owning their new power. Cultural theorists call it "internalized oppression": the deeply ingrained belief among marginalized, disempowered people that we really are not smart enough, good enough or fit to hold power.[11] "I had to tell other [Latino] people we're really talking about power, letting people know that our vote means something," Grace Church's Migdalia Mendez told me. "If you're on the Vestry, you're not just there to listen. You have power, and you can use it to make a difference." As one of the bridge people, she helped to train her peers so they saw themselves as people who could move from the margins to exercise leadership at the heart of the community.

If you are recruiting fresh leaders from marginalized groups, realize these patterns may be at work. Then offer the mentoring and encouragement— and reconfigure your own leadership structures—to make new leaders feel truly, radically welcomed. For example, ask around and see if it would help to change the meeting times: very few non-professional, hourly employees can get away in the middle of the work day, and 6 p.m. on a weekday may exclude a gifted member who works the night shift. Be clear that there is financial assistance for leadership conferences. Go ahead and invite college or graduate students to be Sunday school teachers, knowing they may only be able to commit to one semester at a time. If you need bilingual

---

11. For more on internalized oppression, see Valerie Batts, *Modern Racism: New Melody for the Same Old Tunes* (Cambridge, MA: Episcopal Divinity School Occasional Papers, 1998). www.visions-inc.org.

translation for meetings, help the leaders to get on board, then invest the time and money to make it work well.

Power does not expand of its own accord. But given the genuine commitment and appropriate strategy, it can be shared.

Transforming Your Leadership and Feedback Systems

Take another look at the "Leadership and Feedback Systems" signs and stories in part 2 (pp. 88–92). Then carefully consider these questions:

Where Are We Now?

- What are the key power positions in your congregation? What cultural, racial, age, or economic groups hold those positions?
- Are there power brokers beyond these posts? What groups hold that power?
- Whose leadership do people seem to gravitate toward and trust? Whose leadership is less trusted by the majority of members?
- What are the dominant styles and methods for leadership? What kind of leadership do people most trust? What groups are likely to exercise this kind of authority?
- What are the dominant expectations and requirements for leadership? Think about education, class, experience, longevity, conference attendance, and so on.
- Who is being mentored or nurtured?
- Do your meeting times and locations exclude certain groups from taking part in leadership?
- Whose voice gets heard and honored? Who hears about and influences important decisions?
- Who is being left out of the leadership circle? Are there some common traits or assumptions about these groups of people?
- What is already radically welcoming about your leadership and feedback systems? How will this experience prepare you for the work ahead?

Where Is God Inviting Us to Go?

- How could your leadership—clergy, staff, top lay leaders, committee members—better embrace cultures and groups present in and around the congregation? Be sure to consider formal and informal processes by which people become leaders (i.e., election of vestry members vs. appointments to key committees).

- How could your hiring policies make explicit a commitment to building a radically welcoming congregation?
- How could you mentor and promote leaders from marginalized groups?
- If there is a link between resume/pedigree/wealth and fitness for leadership, how could you sever it? How could you help the congregation to expand its understanding of what is required and useful for leadership?
- How could you expand the community's understanding of the various gifts and skills needed for leadership, so that you honor the gifts and practices of marginalized cultural groups?
- Are there ways to reconfigure certain ministries or leadership bodies so that excluded members could take part?
- How could you open communication lines so that more members have access to information and decision-making processes (even if they are not the ones actually making the decisions)?
- What feedback systems could you put in place to allow more voices to be heard and honored?

Worship

Worship is a community's most important, most accessible public offering. It communicates our values, our culture and our priorities; it shapes us as followers of Christ. As Richard Giles puts it in *Creating Uncommon Worship*, "[The] experience of dying to self, of being reborn, of knowing ourselves to be children of God, is what worship in community should open up to us."[12]

Now imagine if your voice or history were not part of that holy offering. The effect could be devastating and wholly unwelcoming. But reverse that trend, regularly and intentionally include authentic expressions of the culture in which The Other is rooted, and you have just offered a bold welcome to those who have stood on the margins. "We came up with a musical blend: some African-American, some African, some European," said Gary Commins, the former rector at Holy Faith in Inglewood who now serves at St. Luke's Episcopal Church in Long Beach, California. "The point is it's the music and language of people's souls. When you're from a different generation or a different cultural background, and there's nothing from you in the worship, the connection's not going to happen. But hearing (elements of your culture) says there's some of me in here. Even if they don't recognize a song, they know the style. It's something that touches their soul in

---

12. Richard Giles, *Creating Uncommon Worship: Transforming the Liturgy of the Eucharist* (Norwich, England: Canterbury Press, 2004), 12.

An inculturated liturgy invites the different voices present to proclaim the gospel in their own cultural language, and then it listens for ways of crafting a distinctive blend that honors the tradition and the cultural context of members.

a particular way. Now, it's not a matter of someone else's worship; it's *our* worship."

We do not introduce different voices, sounds and styles into the liturgy to make people feel good. We do it because it should be "our" worship, the work of our ancestors within the denominational and community tradition and the work of living members of the assembly who may also bear the gifts of cultures outside the privileged tradition. Especially in the uniquely multicultural American context, we should expect the liturgy to speak of more than the European-American heritage. There is no shame in claiming our role as partners in this work, offering our hearts and voices in all their beauty and particularity to God in worship. There is technically nothing holier or even more elegant, beautiful or transcendent about words, music and images that are printed in a book, at least forty years old, or European.

There are so many ways of faithfully incorporating the voice and presence of The Other into your worship, from Holy Faith's homemade songbook and African procession to the St. Mary's-West Harlem gospel choir. Like St. Bartholomew's-Atlanta, you might enjoy the high-church style of worship but in a way that is consciously accessible. Just add the full worship booklet and a set of friendly greeters who don't make people feel like they're entering a concert hall where they should sit straight and mind their manners (a very culturally specific way of praising God). This field is so full of possibilities—and so important to the dream of radical welcome—that a section of the bibliography is devoted to worship resources for fully embracing people of color, people with disabilities, children and young adults, and gay and lesbian people. Please dive in and let God's dream shape your worship, even as your worship shapes you to live more fully into God's dream.

Some people may complain that such efforts to welcome The Other are distracting or even taking something precious away from those who are already present at the center. With great love, you can explain that actually, people at the center may enjoy and benefit from the expansion of welcome. For instance, they may feel uncomfortable singing gospel or evangelical songs the first few times, but eventually the music may open something inside them. Our most popular service by far at St. Paul's Cathedral in Boston is the Hymn Sing. Twice a year, we pull out *Lift Every Voice and Sing II*, the Episcopal Church's African American hymnal, and let people choose all the music for the service as it proceeds, including an open space for about six songs where the sermon would have gone. People come from all over the diocese and even beyond the Episcopal fold to join the celebration.

One older member, not known for her welcoming attitude, comes up to me probably once a month to say, "I love those old hymns. I wish we could sing them all the time. They just bring you closer to God." So the staff and council decided that, every Sunday, at least one song would come from that hymnal. It has been pure joy.

That said, some efforts to radically welcome in worship may not please certain people at all. In *Holy Hospitality: Worship and the Baptismal Covenant*, Clayton Morris says that's a moment for formation.

> Most Episcopalians recoil at the thought of a presider giving verbal directions during the service. Folks are expected to know what comes next. "That's what inquirers' classes are for!" . . . In order to proclaim the gospel, the church needs to attract people to hear the proclamation. Without a pervasive sense of welcome, people won't come. . . . Seasoned parishioners simply must accommodate the need for a clear sense of welcome in the course of the Sunday morning liturgy.[13]

Is worship for those who are present and empowered? Is it an intimate family affair where everyone knows the rules and all the rote responses, and we hope marginalized people will stay because they would like access to this exclusive club? Or is worship an open and public gathering where we rejoice at the opportunity to welcome the stranger as Christ? Ideally, this should not be an either/or question, but if you have to choose, I pray you will err on the side of The Other.

I say all this knowing full well that, especially among Anglicans, liturgy is the highly charged third rail. The Reverend Susan Deetz, the vocational deacon at St. Paul's in Duluth, Minnesota, understands the dilemma perfectly well. "People want rules. That's why they go to the mega-churches. We only have the Prayer Book to hold us together. You change that, and what's left? Something's got to be stable." Threaten that stability, and you are creeping into treacherous territory.

So let's slow down and look carefully at just what radical welcome has to do with worship. Does liturgical change have to accompany becoming radically welcoming? Shouldn't people have something they can lean on, some constant in an ever-changing world and church? Isn't continuity with centuries of tradition part of our identity, something others will see and love as we do?

First, I would not dream of encouraging any change leaders to begin with major liturgical renewal. You must build trust and carefully discern

---

13. Clayton Morris, *Holy Hospitality: Worship and the Baptismal Covenant* (New York: Church Publishing, 2005), 39–40.

what language and music speaks to those you have gathered and those you hope to gather, and what amount and pace of change the community can tolerate. The fact is, even among the radically welcoming parishes I visited, about half had not recently made major changes in the main Eucharistic liturgy. So the question bears repeating: how do liturgy, radical welcome and the dream of God intersect?

In his essay "On Liturgical Hospitality," William Seth Adams outlines several possible responses to that question.[14]

Assimilation

A popular strategy among mainline churches aims for assimilation, whereby the disempowered one surrenders or downplays his own cultural identity in order to learn and eventually internalize the dominant, often forcefully imposed liturgical practice. The most prominent example of this dynamic is the colonial church planted by Western missionaries around the world. In the Anglican case, such churches may actually place greater value on the maintenance of English culture than their English peers. I will certainly never forget traveling to the Holy Land in 2002 and worshiping at St. George's Cathedral in Jerusalem. The church provided worshipers with a faithful translation of the 1662 Book of Common Prayer, and soon this community of mostly Arab Christians was offering prayers in the King's English with great reverence and solemnity. I wasn't sure what I had just walked into, but I could imagine that any local, non-Anglican entering the church would see the colonial heritage alive and well.

One need not travel to Jerusalem to see this dynamic at work. At a more subtle level, this practice operates whenever congregations invite people to join *if* they demonstrate a willingness to release their home culture and take on the church's received culture and liturgical practices. There is nothing uncommon about assimilation like this; most evangelism efforts assume it.

And yet, it should be stated, not everyone experiences this assimilation as an ill. My friend Alex Dyer, a priest trained in the Episcopal Diocese of New York, has told me of the remarkably diverse Manhattan church where he interned. Anglicans of many classes, races, ages, and sexual orientations were drawn together by their deep love of the awesome, awe-filled liturgy. "They couldn't agree on much, but that was okay," Dyer told me. "They were united in their love for a high, incense-filled liturgy." The key question, for me, was what would happen if someone brought non-European language or music into the church, or if someone not so in love with Mother

---

14. William Seth Adams, "On Liturgical Hospitality," in *Moving the Furniture: Liturgical Theory, Practice and Environment* (New York: Church Publishing Inc., 1999), 87–104.

England walked in. He admitted there would have been no place to hold those alternate visions. While they had a diverse congregation, everyone had gathered around one culture's worship. That is neither multicultural nor radically welcoming.

Acculturation

On the other hand, acculturation assumes a kind of mutual forbearance and even distant appreciation without much movement on either side. We see this model alive in congregations with a parallel worship community that stands alongside the original. For instance, St. Bartholomew's in New York wanted to attract seekers and those burned by prior experience with the church, so for years they offered a relaxed "Come As You Are" service on Sunday evenings, complete with a live band and a praise team that led a contemporary, Catholic-style worship service. That community existed alongside the 11 a.m. crew, the older guard who appreciate being able to continue in their traditional liturgical mode, unaffected by the shifts happening in the evening. They shared the space and joined for some common ministries, but without much interaction as worshiping communities. According to their rector, Bill Tully, that was by design. "We're trying to honor tradition but be radically welcoming. We've worked hard to keep a lot happening under one roof. So you keep the services distinct, and the effect is that it lowers the anxiety level. People are usually worried that one change will trip all sorts of others. Instead, I communicate a conscious sense that we've inherited lots of gifts as a community, *and* we're open to others."

That strategy requires commitment and risk, particularly in a community with a solidly conventional core of people who feel no service in "their" church should depart from the accepted norms. And in communities where the marginalized group has a strong sense of cultural identity—a Spanish-speaking or Nigerian community service or even postmodern young adults—members who have come from the margins may actually prefer having their own worship space. Cultural theorist bell hooks writes with a keen understanding of that yearning: "Those of us who remember living in the midst of racial apartheid know that the separate spaces, the times apart from whiteness, were for sanctuary, for re-imagining and re-membering ourselves. In the past separate space meant down time, time for recovery and renewal."[15] The Right Reverend Cathy Roskam, Bishop Suffragan of the Episcopal Diocese of New York, said she strongly supports parallel development. "Our oneness is in Christ, not in the service. I've no

---

15. Bell hooks, as quoted in Sheryl Kujawa-Holbrook, *A House of Prayer for All Peoples: Building Multiracial Community* (Bethesda, MD: Alban Institute, 2004), 11.

problem with the 8 o'clockers and the 10 o'clockers. Independent worship doesn't have to mean separate communities. There are other things that call people into community. Do a program on spirituality and you'll draw from all the communities."

In many ways, I agree with hooks and Roskam. Space and time apart ought to be guarded and nurtured, not least because people who come from the margins often feel we must be "on" as representatives of our groups. The margins are often the fertile spaces where we come alive and feel at home. And sometimes the marriage of two communities is a power move by the dominant group, which seeks to acquire the marginalized group without sharing power.

Inculturation

But if mutual relationship and embrace is truly happening throughout the community, then the congregation can offer a powerful witness by sitting together and crafting worship that reflects its unique, diverse set of gifts, voices and values. No one will get everything they wanted, but their love for each other and for the living body of Christ compels them to literally lay down some preference at the altar, and instead to listen, celebrate, weep, confess, and pray in the voices of all the people.

That is why the harder task—and perhaps the one that most fully reflects the radically welcoming dream of God in the worshiping body— is inculturation. According to Benedictine Roman Catholic scholar Anscar Chupungco, it is like mutual assimilation. That is,

> [l]iturgical inculturation is basically the assimilation by the liturgy of local cultural patterns. It means that liturgy and culture share the same pattern of thinking, speaking, and expressing themselves through rites, symbols and artistic forms. In short, the liturgy is inserted into the culture, history and tradition of the people among whom the Church dwells. It begins to think, speak, and ritualize according to the local cultural pattern.[16]

In a multicultural context—and most American congregations are situated in a multicultural setting, no matter how dominant one race, generation or class may seem—an inculturated liturgy would reflect the various local patterns present. It does *not* surrender all the traditions that have shaped and held the community or denominational body through history (this would simply be one-way assimilation in the reverse direction). But it also doesn't assume these practices will resonate with The Other (or even with members of the privileged group). It invites the different voices present to

---

16. Anscar Chupungco, as cited in Adams, "On Liturgical Hospitality," 90.

proclaim the gospel in their own cultural language, and then it listens for ways of crafting a distinctive blend that honors the tradition *and* the cultural context of members.

Professor and pastor Kathy Black calls this "culturally-conscious worship."[17] According to Black, this form of worship "intentionally works with a consciousness of 1) our multiracial, multiethnic, and multicultural society and world; 2) the cultural diversity (its gifts and challenges) present in the congregation; and 3) persons who experience living on the margins and living with inequity of power." To do it, we must cultivate a trust and openness of heart that most traditions have frankly shied from. To do

> Online Extra: Assessment Tool for Studying Your Congregation's Reality and Charting Your Dream

it, especially for Episcopalians, many of us will have to refine our definition of what it means to be Anglican, since that identity has been so closely tied to particular formulations of the Prayer Book liturgy. If we accept that invitation, we will find ourselves in good company. After all, it was Archbishop of Canterbury Rowan Williams who asserted that "there is plenty of theological room for diversity of rhythm and style, so long as we have ways of identifying the same living Christ at the heart of every expression of Christian life in common."[18]

That is the unique call of worship. If we cannot examine our liturgy and music and how they embrace or exclude, inspire or threaten, stagnate or breathe, then we have thrown up a roadblock to welcome—and to the movement of the Holy Spirit.

Transforming Your Worship

Take another look at "Worship" signs and stories in part 2 (pp. 92–94). Then carefully consider these questions:

Where Are We Now?

- What is the lived purpose of liturgy and music in your congregation? What do people tend to experience, share, learn, or encounter?
- What are the expectations regarding liturgy and music? How should it be conducted? Who should be involved?

---

17. Kathy Black, *Culturally-Conscious Worship* (St. Louis, MO: Chalice Press, 2000), 12. Black intentionally differentiates this culturally conscious worship from *multicultural* worship, which happens in a community with several cultures present but primarily reflects the dominant power group's values and culture.

18. Archbishop's Council, *Mission-Shaped Church: Church Planting and Fresh Expressions of Church in a Changing Context* (London: Church House Publishing, 2004), vii.

- How does worship look and feel? If there is more than one service, focus on the one that is best-attended and/or the one most of the church's key leaders attend. Whose cultural and aesthetic values shape the worship? Whose voice, image or presence shows up less often, if at all, in worship?

  - Is your worship accessible to people who do not know your traditions? How would someone who is new to the church find out what words to speak, where to go to receive Communion, when or why to stand or sit or take part in other communal gestures?
  - Do you have greeters? What is their purpose? How do they function?
  - What is already radically welcoming about your worship? How will this prepare you for the work ahead?

Where Is God Inviting Us to Go?

- How could your liturgy and music reflect the dream of God for your community?
- What would it communicate about your community's culture(s), values and mission?
- How could the language, symbols, readings, music, preaching, physical movement, and other elements reflect a wider range of cultures, generations or classes?
- How could you craft liturgies that are not quite so "controlled and contained" but sometimes "threaten to leap off the page and bite us?"[19] How might you accomplish this goal faithfully, responsibly and effectively, continuing to craft "good" liturgy?
- How could you include different gifts and values without misappropriation—that is, making sure you don't incorporate cultural traditions without either seeking relationship with the community of origin or at least sharing the background and story of that community?
- How could you ensure the full participation and welcome of people new to the tradition and to your church, especially people who come with the experience of being marginalized by the groups that hold power in your church?
- How could you introduce fresh music and liturgical forms in ways that are inspiring and least threatening to your members?

---

19. Giles, *Creating Uncommon Worship*, 12.

GO DEEPER . . .

- Which of the stories, comments or ideas you just read was the most challenging? Exciting? How do they connect with your own story? What do they inspire you to ask or to do?
- How do these reflections link with your church's story or the stories of churches you've known?
- What might radical welcome look like in your community? Write some thoughts or even draw a picture. Take these considerations into account:

  — Who is "The Other" for your community?

  — Whose voice and culture would challenge or disrupt the way things have been? (Don't just think ideology, but think especially of groups systemically oppressed and disempowered by the church and society. A hint: you will surely think of more than one group.)

  — How would your congregational life change if the groups now on the margins came closer to help to shape your common life?

- Look at the five areas of your congregational life and the suggestions and strategies in each. Where has your community already begun this work? Where is your community most ready to make fresh moves? What is the deeper work that you would eventually take on over a longer term?

Check Your Reality

Most congregations can grow, if they can live into the idea
of radical welcome. You have to examine what's under
the iceberg, what militates against transformation, for it
to happen. You have to make some conscious choices.

THE RIGHT REVEREND CATHY ROSKAM,
EPISCOPAL DIOCESE OF NEW YORK

There's the dream, sitting in front of you, so real you can almost touch it.
Then you reach out, and it shimmers and fades.

With such fervent hope stirring us, why can't we just make the changes
to become radically welcoming? Why does it feel as if we are running our
legs ragged but moving only an inch? Why does it seem there is a block bigger than any single person or even congregation that's standing between us
and the dream?

Because there is.

Every church has a history and a cultural identity. It is the water you swim
in, the air all around you. Chances are, this story and these assumptions have
been around much longer than your current congregation. These forces surround, and sometimes even contradict, whatever you are doing on the ground
to welcome The Other. Part of welcoming *radically* is paying attention to
these chilling forces. It's knowing how people feel when they come through
your door and why certain groups might never even come near, no matter
how welcoming and friendly you feel you are. It's knowing your history, knowing your culture, knowing the aura that floats around you and shades everything you say and do, how it's hampering and how it could help you.

In this chapter, I invite you to practice wrapping your mind around your
church's culture and practices. Our test case is the Episcopal Church in
the United States. If you're not Episcopalian, don't skip too quickly: notice

the questions and patterns, and then delve deep and dig for the inherited, inherent blocks to the fulfillment of God's dream in your own church. Radical welcome seeks to transform these blocks and build a liberative community in their place. You can only do that once you get to know what's really going on—and what others see that you never even noticed.

What Are "They" Saying About "Us"?

Q: How many Episcopalians does it take to change a light bulb?

A: Three: One to call the electrician, one to mix the drinks, and another to stand on the side complaining about how much better the old one was.

A friend forwarded this joke to me via e-mail several years ago. At the time, I was a fairly new Episcopalian and wondered what journey I had just signed on for. Because even if it was a joke, and I could guffaw out loud with the best of 'em, I knew it was also a cultural artifact capturing something about our hyper class consciousness and rigid resistance to change. On some level, this joke told the story about how others view my church.

For most Episcopalians, that's not reality. However, it's what a lot of people think of us. And if we take a moment—an honest, self-appraising moment—we have to admit that much of the history and cultural inheritance that define our congregations, dioceses and denominational identity remain rooted in this elitist pattern.

Sheryl Kujawa-Holbrook knows this only too well. As a key proponent for anti-racism and a professor at the Episcopal Divinity School, teaching the history and polity of the Church along with pastoral care and Christian education, she has thought a lot about Episcopalians and change. "You've got to consider patterns of power and privilege," she told me. "As Episcopalians, we have a history of holding power, so talking change gets complicated. People may be excited about inclusion and diversity, but when you talk about changing power dynamics and systems, few people stay excited."

The idea of broadening our cultural base—or the idea that anyone would come along who did not seek to assimilate to the church's practices and traditions as received—has rarely occurred to Episcopalians. Susan Deetz, the deacon at St. Paul's in Duluth, helped me to understand why. "The church used to be the institution that taught you how to fit with the culture," said Deetz, a cradle Episcopalian. "If you didn't want the culture, then you wouldn't want the church." Assimilation was assumed, especially for immigrants trying to find their place in a new land, and next to public schools, the church was the chief assimilating institution that helped to broker that process.

That's not always a negative. But it can be, especially when membership in a church gets viewed as the equivalent of leaving your own culture behind. When other black, working-class friends and family found out I was becoming an Episcopalian, I took lots of flack. "Why are you joining *that* church?" people wanted to know. One person thought she had the answer: "I always knew you were sididdy. This just proves it." Mind you, a "sididdy" person is one who thinks she is better than others in her group. And in communities the world over, certainly in the Americas, the Episcopal Church is often viewed as the church for people who think they are better than everyone else. It's the church of the high-society black folks, the ones who are lighter-skinned, better-educated, with their emotions and color under control. The church of the house slave, rather than the church of the field slave.

> The fault lines here are intellectual lines. There's a huge bias toward being analytical, brighter than the average bear. Anything not to seem like the fundamentalists.
>
> MAGGIE KULYK,
> ST. BARTHOLOMEW'S-ATLANTA

As I've spoken with other people of color and people from less-privileged class backgrounds, as well as gay and lesbian folks and young adults, many have reported similar experiences. We know better than most that the Episcopal Church has often been the church of choice for people who want some of *that:* some power, some culture, some social training, some privilege, even if it was privilege by association. If people assimilated to this church's culture, if they proved they could be "proper," then they were rewarded with a boost up the social ladder. In order to effect deep change, we will have to reckon with the skewed power dynamics and classist, Euro-American cultural dependency that has limited the Episcopal Church and most other mainline churches for far too long.

The Church of the Empire

Americans find it easy to gloss over or just forget, but the Episcopal Church is the church planted by an empire. And while our church is more democratic than most of our counterparts in the Anglican Communion, we still bear the marks of our founding. The church of empire was supposed to secure order, quell revolution, advance reason. Let the Baptists have their wild times. Let the Catholics be "ethnic." We had to keep it together, because we had to rule a nation. Never veer too far to the left or right. We had to wield power with a steady hand and a cool head.

The truth is, from its birth in 1529, when King Henry VIII declared himself the head of the Church throughout his empire, the Church of England has struggled to chart a course toward the center and to fulfill its call to maintain order for the whole. When Queen Elizabeth I ascended to the throne in the second half of the sixteenth century, she saw a nation ripped by the bitter and violent disputes between Protestants and Catholics. Religion was the chief rallying point for the parties. Elizabeth immediately realized the fate of the realm depended on constructing a compromise. "Queen Elizabeth said religion shouldn't fragment people," Kujawa-Holbrook explained. "She wanted to put together a tradition that most people would be able to follow and fit into." And so she did, crafting an ideological and theological middle path, known as the Elizabethan Settlement (or Compromise) that for a time brought warring parties to heel. Another of her more severe peacemaking ventures, the Act of Uniformity of 1559, imposed harsh penalties on anyone who did not adhere to the Book of Common Prayer's precise prescriptions for worship in the church.

It is impossible to understand these ostensibly religious developments apart from their political implications in England and abroad. Elizabeth was a faithful woman, but she also knew an established church with a rigorously enforced, common tradition could help bring a sober, orderly calm upon the people. That was the church's chief calling in England.

It was also the church's mission in colonies throughout the so-called New World, even after the American Revolution. True, the framers for the new American church instituted democratic systems and independence from the Crown (including removing prayers for the monarch and axing the requirement that ordained leaders vow allegiance to the monarch).[1] All that said, the church in America was still a church of the governing and owning class and, in many places, the masters' class. These leaders had a vested interest in maintaining order, reasonable rule and social stability, and they were highly suspicious of anything that smacked of emotion, renewal or revolution in the church.

It should not surprise us, then, that even before the Revolution, as the Great Awakening swept the nation in the mid-1700s, Anglicans in America hesitated to jump on board. How ironic that an Anglican clergyman from England, George Whitefield, was the one stirring up much of the cross-denominational fervor. While his colleagues in America first welcomed their English brother, the reception soured when they saw how he stirred passions and inspired change wherever he went. According to Episcopal Church historian Robert Pritchard, most Anglican clergy beheld the awakened, spirit-filled masses with great disdain.[2] Especially in New England,

---

1. This historical account is drawn from Robert Pritchard's *A History of the Episcopal Church* (Harrisburg, PA: Morehouse Publishing, 1999).

2. Ibid., 55.

where Anglicans had little strength before the Great Awakening, the church made a name for itself by providing shelter for horrified Congregationalists and Presbyterians whose churches had welcomed the spirit of revival. The Anglican tradition was aligned more closely with the Enlightenment, or the Age of Reason, and thus grounded itself in Scripture, tradition and reason. Converts could trust that this church's liturgy, practices and theology would always appeal to the stable, rational mind, and not to the turbulent emotions and extremism of their awakened, but not enlightened, peers.

> Decorum has been highly valued in Episcopal circles. . . . As cultural diversity alters the way communities understand decency and order, the look, feel and sound of the assembly changes, but there is always a quiet sense of discomfort among Episcopalians if things seem a bit loose.
>
> CLAYTON MORRIS, *HOLY HOSPITALITY*

That snapshot only begins to explain how the culture of the Episcopal Church has been shaped by its call to maintain social order and stability. As the church of the establishment (if not the established church), Anglicanism in the United States has been steeped in owning-class, elite, northern European culture, which demands that people maintain rigid control of their emotions, actions, words, bodies, and environment in order to prove their superior fitness to hold power.[3]

Even when the people in the pews are members of a marginalized community, that does not guarantee they will bring a different cultural attitude to bear. Sometimes, it is quite the opposite, as one report from the Lambeth 1988 Conference remarks:

> [W]hen Anglicanism was exported to other continents, it came not only with the "Englishness" of certain styles of clothing, music and worship, but with certain assumptions about who made decisions, who had authority in social life, who had ultimate control in economic affairs, markets, production, land ownership. The dominance of the English style . . . could be seen as a reflection of the plain facts of political and economic dominance.[4]

As a result of that dominance, Kwok Pui Lan points out, people in former colonial strongholds discovered that participating in the dominant Anglo-Anglican culture gave them a social and economic boost. She has noticed that

---

3. For a thorough examination of the concept of "whiteness," white racial identity and the interlocking issues of class privilege and heterosexual and male privilege, and an honest appraisal of the costs of privilege, see Mary Elizabeth Hobgood's *Dismantling Privilege: An Ethics of Accountability* (Cleveland, OH: Pilgrim Press, 2000).

4. Kwok Pui Lan, *The Truth Shall Make You Free: The Lambeth Conference 1988* (London: Church House Publishing, 1988), 88.

Anglican churches in many parts of the world remain cultural representations of the colonial era. Africans and Asians living in tropical climates continue to wear English clerical dress, even under the hot blazing sun. The African bishop is addressed as the Lord Bishop of Cape Coast or Freetown. . . . In many cases, such mimicry of the "Mother Church" serves not as a mockery of colonial authority, but as a sign of privilege by association.[5]

Though North Americans are loathe to acknowledge our own colonial heritage, it continues to operate powerfully. I sat one afternoon to discuss these issues with Brother Geoffrey Tristram, a member of the Society of St. John the Evangelist, a monastic order based in Cambridge, Massachusetts. Born, raised and priested in England, Brother Geoffrey has thought a lot about the American church and why we hold so fervently to a language and tradition that are not home-grown. "Americans are obsessed, it seems to me, with questions of identity," he said. "They desperately want to belong to something and to find their identity in that. Especially if they're Anglicans, that becomes their cultural identity. They can be a part of something. It is their home."

And so, for many Episcopalians, including the converts, we want the eighteenth-century hymns because they are part of our adopted cultural heritage. We want language that sounds formal and elevated (read: British) because it gives us a connection to something that sounds venerable and, by extension, holy and transcendent. We want a Prayer Book liturgy with little variation because it helps us to feel grounded in something that has "always" been this way (remember that, until 1979, nearly all Episcopal churches used one form for the Eucharist, and its language had changed little in several centuries). This complex cultural heritage acts like gravity, holding the church close to the ground and, in many instances, locking it in place. If leaders shift any part of that cultural complex—even with the hope of embracing emerging generations, different ethnic groups, oppressed sexual minorities, or people from less privileged class backgrounds—the repercussions can be dire.

Adding to the burden, we've also been appointed conservator of English-American identity by many non-Episcopalians. In particular, the language

> Each one of us lives with particular images and understandings of the church, many of which strengthen, console and challenge us. In some instances, these images make it difficult to recognize the presence of God's larger purposes and radically reordering love.
>
> THE MOST REVEREND FRANK T. GRISWOLD, "A WORD TO THE CHURCH FROM THE PRESIDING BISHOP," JUNE 23, 2004.

---

5. Kwok Pui Lan, "The Legacy of Cultural Hegemony in the Anglican Church," in *Beyond Colonial Anglicanism: The Anglican Communion in the 21st Century*, ed. Ian Douglas and Kwok Pui Lan (New York: Church Publishing Inc., 2001), 56–57.

of the Prayer Book has taken on cultural icon status. Gregory Howe saw various non-Episcopalian critics weigh in following the 1979 Prayer Book revision, including William F. Buckley Jr., publisher of the *National Review*. These protectors of the tradition, Howe said,

> try to freeze us in place at a late stage of the 1928 Prayer Book, as though we are custodians of a sacred cultural icon without which Anglo civilization, as we know it, would wither away. . . . For them the Episcopal Church is the guardian of an exquisitely beautiful museum piece.

Although he serves as Custodian of the Book of Common Prayer for the Episcopal Church, Howe is not satisfied with the calling to preserve the liturgy in amber so that future generations can gaze upon it with reverence and awe. He knows the liturgy—and the Church—has a higher calling than that of "museum-keeper." "What does [preservation] have to do with the imperatives of the Gospel?" he asks. "Aren't we sending the message that spreading the Gospel isn't quite as important to us as the beautiful, even glorious literature (and other magnificent treasures) entrusted to us?"[6]

It seems that is precisely the message many people want and even demand that we send. So we take on the role of conservator and standard bearer of good taste, shouldering the white man's burden, proclaiming to the world our commitment to a firm, unchanging identity.

A Liberating Legacy

If that were the whole story for the Episcopal Church, we would be in dire trouble. The truth—the whole truth—is that there are many gifts already in our knapsack designed to equip us for radical welcome. While we need to understand how our culture militates against new life, we also need to celebrate and move to center stage the resources and practices that position us well for transformational growth.

For instance, as much as the Anglican tradition in America spurns certain change (particularly in the liturgy and the definition of our cultural identity), we also share a theological tradition that prepares us to take risks and to sit with contraries and hard truths. True, we have been the church of the establishment, preaching sobriety and order throughout the world. But we are also the church of the *via media*, able to hold tensions and seeming

---

6. Gregory Howe, "Expansive Language in Cyberspace" in *Gleanings: Essays on Expansive Language*, ed. Ruth Meyers and Phoebe Pettingell (New York: Church Publishing Inc., 2001), 49–50.

contradictions with the hope that there is always a third way, a way that is complex and even complicated but true to reality and context.

Our church was founded not as the people of the Prayer Book or a single liturgy (as we have seen, the crackdown and severe enforcement came later, in the wake of political strife). We are the people who demand that all believers be allowed to consciously, faithfully discern the mind of God, and the corollary is that no one—especially no single cultural or generational group—has a lock on the truth or the form in which it can be expressed.

American theologian William Porcher DuBose, a nineteenth-century evangelical apologist for slavery who also defended the Confederacy on the battlefield, still understood the Anglican necessity to gather and honor many voices and perspectives in order to grasp God's truth in its fullness.

> All the truth of the church is not yet mine. There are points of it that I know to be true, because I have been all the time approximating to them, but I am still waiting, and shall probably die waiting, for them to become true to me. Truth is not an individual thing; no one of us has it all—even all of it that is known. Truth is a corporate possession, and the knowledge of it is a corporate process[7]

> I'll tell you now: this class thing is going to bite at us again and again. The people in power are still privileged people. And that's a deadly combination: upper-class, individualistic, comfortable faith. The Episcopal Church needs the community of the poor and oppressed. It would be so easy for us to fall, because we're so privileged.
>
> ERIC LAW, EPISCOPAL DIOCESE OF LOS ANGELES

Following in the footsteps of Anglican theologians like Richard Hooker, DuBose knew that we need one another and the bits and scraps of truth and love each of us brings to the holy banquet table.

Likewise, in the church's earliest documents, the framers have acknowledged the complexity and multiplicity of life, and pledged that this church would respond with care to those changing times. The preface to the 1662 Prayer Book declares the early church's hope "to keep the mean between the two extremes, of too much stiffness in refusing, and too much easiness in admitting any variation from it." While these leaders would never encourage change just to make things interesting, they also admitted that the actual forms of worship are "things in their own nature indifferent, and alterable." For that reason, "according to the various exigency of times and occasions, such changes and alterations should be made therein, as to those that are in place

---

7. William Porcher DuBose, *Turning Points in My Life* (1912), as reprinted in Richard Schmidt, *Glorious Companions: Five Centuries of Anglican Spirituality* (Grand Rapids, MI: Eerdmans, 2002), 205.

of Authority should from time to time seem either necessary or expedient." For centuries the Anglican tradition has encouraged leaders to discern what forms of worship would actually reach and edify people in their context, and to build bridges accordingly.

And lest we think that commitment stalled before crossing the Atlantic, we need only look to the Articles of Religion, a non-binding set of statements about the faith adopted by the American church in 1801, where the authors wrote: "It is not necessary that traditions and ceremonies be in all places one, or utterly like; for at all times they have been diverse, and may be changed according to the diversity of countries, times and men's manners, so that nothing be ordained against God's Word."[8] In short, the church's architects were wise enough to make room for the natural, inevitable, even desirable translation of the liturgy and doctrine into the cultural language of the people who use it, as long as the movement is consonant with Scripture. The change must be discerned by a community in response to their context and in relationship with their bishop, and not by rogue individualists. Having met that criteria, the community may move forward trusting they remain true to the tradition.

And it makes perfect sense that the American church's leaders would have made provision for that sort of change. The great move that marked the birth of Anglicanism was simply this: translating the Catholic, Latin liturgy and tradition so that it spoke to the hearts of the English people. Thomas Cranmer, who wrote that first Prayer Book and secured his place as the father of Anglicanism, set the precedent in the mid 1500s. Every time we translate our liturgy so that it speaks in the language of the people, or open our church to the culture, voices, music, practices of The Other in our midst, we are walking in Cranmer's footsteps. That is why Leonel Mitchell, widely respected leader of the movement that gave us the newest Prayer Book in 1979, could say with such confidence

We do Cranmer and his work no honor by gilding it and putting it on display. We best follow the lead of the first Book of Common Prayer by making liturgy in our own day, for our own people. It is not an heirloom of our cultural heritage to be displayed in a showcase for our children to admire; it is a working tool to be used by us and by them.[9]

---

8. Book of Common Prayer, 874.

9. Mitchell, as quoted in Phoebe Pettingell, "I Hear America Praying: Liturgy, the American Vernacular ad Expansive Language," in *Gleanings: Essays on Expansive Language*, ed. Ruth Meyers and Phoebe Pettingell (New York: Church Publishing Inc., 2001), 21.

"Anglican identity" can be code for something else. I think it's code for "niche church." It usually means worship one way. It has musical, liturgical and building implications.

CHARLES FULTON, CONGREGATIONAL DEVELOPMENT OFFICER, EPISCOPAL CHURCH CENTER

Daniel Caballero, formerly the Episcopal Church Center's Officer for Hispanic Congregational Ministries, agrees wholeheartedly with Mitchell. He told me the primacy of the vernacular was part of what drew him to the Episcopal Church, and it's why he has hope that in time we can be a church that welcomes all people. "The Episcopal Church stands for, was formed for, the common people. The Book of Common Prayer came because the services and instruction had been in Latin, and they wanted to expand it and make it for the common people. It is only common once it has been translated into your language. And I mean cultural translation, not just linguistic."

Comments like Caballero's represent more than wishful thinking for Anglicans. They are part of our reality.

What's Your Congregational Reality?

Every congregation, every denomination, every tradition possesses just such a rich, sometimes contradictory story. These are the blessings and challenges that make us who we are, the gifts and liabilities we carry along every step of the journey toward radical welcome. Only by acknowledging them *in tota* can we strategize smart for the road ahead.

To get at those issues, some congregations opt for a systemic assessment. St. Bartholomew's in New York hired former All Saints-Pasadena rector George Regas as a consultant to study the congregation and its reality and then guide them through the visioning and planning process. "We needed to know, What are some of the obstacles to growth?" St. Bart's Rector Bill Tully explained. "Imagine a length with spikes on it, created to keep the pigeons from coming. We didn't invent it, but it's there. For us, that length is the perceptions, the traditions, the architecture."

You may take advantage of user-friendly resources like those in Studying Congregations: A New Handbook and The Inviting Church: A Study of New Member Assimilation,[10] both of which detail processes that congregations can employ to study themselves effectively. You may also decide to

---

10. Nancy Ammerman, Jackson Carroll, Carl Dudley, and William McKinney, eds., *Studying Congregations: A New Handbook* (Nashville: Abingdon, 1998); and Roy Oswald and Speed Leas, *The Inviting Church: A Study of New Member Assimilation* (Bethesda, MD: Alban Institute, 1987).

take a more informal survey, speaking with old-timers, newcomers, former members, and neighbors to get a sense of what the congregation actually communicates about itself.

Trinity Church in Boston launched a major assessment and revisioning process prior to calling its latest rector. They set up committees of lay leaders who dove into the parish and into the community to do deep listening. While there, they heard some hard truths: many people inside the church felt disconnected and marginalized; meanwhile, other churches and civic leaders saw them as "the 800-pound gorilla" that always wants to control whatever it touches; the insulated, intellectual castle with no desire to engage The Other. Those leaders remembered times that Trinity had stepped out for social change, and what a difference the parish had

> Online Extra: Assessment Tool for Studying Your Congregation's Reality and Charting Your Dream

made; they only wished the church's leaders would come out of their rarefied environs more often. When Trinity hired its next rector, they hired a woman with a track record for leading large, urban churches into deeper relationship with their neighbors.

That's smart strategy, informed by knowledge. And it's knowledge gained by going out and asking the right questions.

How do you create a framework to hold this delicate conversation about the congregation's systems and deep cultural patterns? Invite a team of leaders to spearhead the listening process (if there is a vision team guiding the process of discernment around radical welcome, even better). You could also ask an outside leader to come and perform the assessment with you. The "Where Are We Now?" sets of queries posted throughout the "Re-Imagine Your Common Life" chapter will help you to examine the contours of your congregation's common life with radical welcome in mind, moving through mission, identity, ministries and relationships, leadership, and worship.

As you listen and construct the picture of your congregation's common life, take note of the dominant patterns and strongest impressions. Imagine what someone who didn't know you well would see and think first. Because if you want to connect with those who've been systemically, historically held at the margins of your church, there is no way to get there without understanding the congregation's reality in terms of power, privilege, oppression, insiders, and outsiders. The goal is not to stir guilt and remorse, though both may surface over time. Rather, this kind of truth-telling equips you with the information you need in order to craft an effective, compassionate strategy. You can build on strengths and carefully note growing edges before they cut you or The Other you hope to radically welcome.

GO DEEPER . . .

- Which of the stories, comments or ideas you just read was the most challenging? Exciting? How do they connect with your own story? What do they inspire you to ask or to do?

- How do these reflections link with your church's story, or the stories of churches you've known?

- Create a parish timeline. When was your congregation most alive? What did the neighborhood look like? How did the church connect with the community? What has changed in the church's vitality? How has the relationship with the neighborhood shifted?

- Think of the stereotypes and the cultural inheritance attached to your tradition and your congregation. What are the greatest challenges to radical welcome in your congregational and denominational history? How does your history and reality actually equip you for transformation and radical welcome?

- In what ways does your church send a culturally exclusive message? Who might walk to your door, or enter your church on a Sunday, and not feel valued or visible? Picture the outcasts, the strangers, The Other who has been systemically oppressed and disempowered in society and in the wider church.

- Return to the five-part image of the church's bodylife: its mission and vision, identity, ministries and relationships, leadership and feedback systems, and worship. What elements of your church's bodylife are the most entrenched and least welcoming? Where have you begun to move toward the dream?

Reckon with Your Fear

When we ask people to change, we're going into
their deepest programming. Every individual
has an iceberg—which you see above—
and below are the myths, patterns. Even though
most change is external, people are afraid of what
it will do to their internal world, their iceberg.
They see change, they feel threatened.
If you change this, *will I disappear*?

THE REVEREND ERIC LAW, EPISCOPAL DIOCESE OF LOS ANGELES

The "F" Word

Call it what you like—resistance, anxiety, hesitation, paralysis, defensiveness—fear is always with us, and perhaps never more than when the world and the systems that have anchored us start to change. Your community may fervently hope to become radically welcoming. You may have already begun to identify the specific changes you would like to implement, and you're sure others in your congregation will be excited about joining the march. But consider changes like these, and imagine the response:

- hearing fewer of the community's beloved traditional hymns every Sunday
- mounting plaques or art representing the aesthetic values and images of non-dominant groups
- creating slots on the worship rota specifically for under-represented groups and reducing the number for others

- holding two slots on the Church Council for minority ethnic groups or homeless members or gay and lesbian leaders
- offering bilingual translation at meetings
- installing a screen and investing in a projector for alternative worship
- requiring that all ministries rise from the common mission and not just pet projects

Especially when our cherished institutions and private communities are "threatened" with change, it is quite natural to recoil, hunker down and resist like hell. Church leaders everywhere told me this struggle had probably sapped more of their energy and sabotaged more of their efforts than almost anything else. Yet, we have so little equipment or language for naming and delving into that fear. In some congregations, there may even be outright resistance to speaking of something so "personal" and "intimate" as fear and pain. In these places, people keep quiet lest they look like they're trying to use church as group therapy. Of course, professional intervention has its place. But surely the church can provide the space for admitting and holding the fear and pain we experience as transformation occurs within our faith lives and communities.

So how do you tell hesitant parishioners church will now challenge them, setting out a radical vision that may differ from so much of what they've worked to maintain? How do you help them—and yourself—to hold and eventually to transform fear? You can begin by getting to know the nature and sources of fear, particularly the fear of The Other and the fear of change.

Fear of The Other

Anyone would feel a bit uncomfortable in the presence of someone whose perspective, practices, history, hopes, even their looks and smell, seem at least on the surface—and perhaps even after some exploration—dramatically different from your own. Even if you find it exciting to experience new cultures, some of the rush is surely the anxiety of approaching the unknown, the out-of-the-ordinary, the marginal. Why else do we call someone new and different a "stranger"? They are, to some degree, strange.

I am wary when people say, "If you just get to know people, you realize we're really all the same underneath." Actually, we are *and* we're not. We all hurt, but different things cause us pain. We all laugh, but different things make us laugh. We all celebrate beauty, but what is beautiful in one culture may be a shock to the system or dull and lifeless in another. We all hope for some measure of success and peace, but defining that from one context to the next is like shooting at a moving target. Difference is difference. Expecting to transform The Other into a familiar commodity ignores the reality and value of variation and difference. It begs the deviation to be absorbed once again into a norm that we get to name and craft—usually in something like our own image.

Of course we find ourselves anxious in relationship with the one who is Other to us, and particularly the marginalized, oppressed Other. It's more than disagreement, more than encountering the great unknown. This person's very presence reminds us of—and perhaps represents some fundamental threat to—our own unearned privilege. Oppressive systems have taught us that there is something threatening, something ugly, out there, and then they have constructed The Other as a human repository for much of that ugliness. In the extreme, that can lead to horrible responses like gay-bashing, lashing out at "welfare mothers," or placing a quarter of black men in jail to keep the streets safe. More subtle forms of fear and prejudice pulse not so far under the surface, taking privileged people just a little off center whenever they're confronted with the specter of The Other.

> I know what some folks think when they see me [a homeless man]. I get the funny vibes. I said okay, and I went to another member to get some counsel. She got it right away and said, "Honey, don't you worry about it. God is not afraid of you."
>
> CHARLES KELLY,
> ST. MARY'S-WEST HARLEM

Even members of oppressed groups look across to those in our own groups with some measure of fear. Anti-oppression experts call this horizontal oppression, when oppression flows not just on a vertical axis, from the privileged down to the oppressed, but also on a horizontal axis, from one oppressed person against another, and sometimes within the oppressed person herself. We've bought the oppressors' line and projected those assumptions onto each other and ourselves.

Fear of The Other is so primal, so powerful. It resides deeper than most of us know or would want to admit. It silently telegraphs tension and negative energy into almost any encounter between insiders and outsiders. It's there, begging to be named, held and somehow cracked open.

Fear of Change

Hardly any experience inspires fear quite like change. Much of our fear of other groups, new experiences and the great unknown can be traced, I would wager, to the fear of change. As humans, we instinctively seek stability and avoid pain and possible rejection. If some experience might prompt pain, loss, failure, or rejection, we are apt to construct our lives and institutions to avoid the cause and thus to keep that pain at bay. In the process, we can easily begin to read nearly all change as a source of suffering, or some deterioration from a better, safer, original state.

The fear of change is a powerful and pervasive thing. All the more reason to pause and take a brief systematic look at this phenomenon on four key levels.[1] Look carefully, because our fear of change in one realm might be rooted in or intimately linked to fear at some other level.

1. **Personal:** At the personal level, we tend to fear anything that shifts us out of our own centered identity (unless it is a shift we choose— losing weight, building self-esteem, shifting to a higher-wage job). Lurking beneath this fear, on some level, is an intense suspicion that personal change will lead to hurt or even annihilation.

2. **Interpersonal:** The same fear operates at an interpersonal level: a good relationship is stable, predictable and, ultimately, unchanging. If we grow, we must grow together. Otherwise, it seems we've been abandoned or rejected and left to fend for ourselves.

3. **Institutional:** An organization and its members can certainly experience the fear of change. Many of us turn to our churches precisely because they provide a quasi-family within which we can pretend things have "always been this way." If new people, new ideas, new practices arrive, they threaten the sense of safety, order and meaning the institution provided. If this institution changes, how will we orient ourselves in the world?

4. **Cultural:** For many of us, change associated with the foundational principles that make up a culture—like God and the church—inspires the greatest fear. If God changes, then the world might as well turn in on itself. Nothing is sure. Even if the change is in the church, its doctrines or its practices, we may sense the creep toward some dreaded third rail: tampering with that which has no beginning and no end and should endure for all ages. Deep inside, I would suggest, there lurks the supreme fear: "If the way I understand God, or what God has revealed in Scripture and in the church, could change, does any of it even matter? Will all this change rip away my connection to God, or possibly erase God altogether?" No wonder we are far more likely to skirt that kind of pain and change whenever possible.

---

1. I have borrowed the model for performing analysis on these four levels from Valerie Batts, founder and executive director of Visions Inc., an Arlington, Massachusetts–based consulting firm that guides institutions toward becoming anti-racist and multicultural. For more information on Visions, go to http://www.visions-inc.com or call (781) 643-5190.

You can see now why mainline churches' recent battles over liturgical renewal, sexuality and cultural identity have been so fraught with tension. Although people may be resisting particular innovations, that's only part of the story. As Kujawa-Holbrook reminded me, "Making change—even what some of us think of as simple change—can cause people personal pain. For instance, the language of certain liturgies marks the special moments in their lives. It is why people who wouldn't ordinarily go near Jacobean English ask for the King James Version of Psalm 23 at funerals. At those pivotal moments, the affective dimension takes over."

Some call this the "language of the heart": the language that suddenly transports you to a special place, communicates the holy, and links you to tradition and your very own communion of the saints. It is a verbal language, and a musical language. It is also a visual, liturgical, physical, cultural language. Tamper with it—even for the best of reasons—and you should not be surprised at the jerk of fear, resistance and pain.

> I admit it: I get disturbed at the noon Spanish-language service.
> All the children running about. Not knowing their language makes it tougher.
> I don't know what to do.
>
> PAULINE MESSER,
> GRACE CHURCH-LAWRENCE

The Sound of Fear

People will rarely come out and say, "I'm scared" or "I don't want *them* around." Our fear morphs and takes on many voices: the voice of scarcity, the voice of hesitation, the voice of anxiety, the voice of defensiveness. Listening for the sound of fear takes great care. Many of the people I met in the course of the Radical Welcome Project were brave enough to share their own fears and the fears they encountered. In so many cases, a reasonable, innocuous comment cloaks a deep fear and an old story.

> There's a real fear that we'd have to dumb down to attract people of color. People say things like,
> "How would Spanish speakers understand our sermons?"
>
> JIM WHITE, ALL SAINTS-PASADENA

As you consider the list that follows, realize that there is nothing inherently wrong with many of these comments. The trouble comes when we allow the reservations to go unexamined and thus to cover deeper fears below the surface.

- *But I come here to feel good and safe. Is that so wrong?*
  The fear of losing our comfort zone

- *I hope they don't expect us to change our liturgy.*
  The fear of losing a venerable tradition

- *It's not a judgment—they're just not like us.*
  The fear of losing a community's cultural, social identity
- *But shouldn't we study it a little more? We've never done this before.*
  The fear of looking or being judged ignorant, unprepared or otherwise less than "together"
- *What if we mess it up?*
  The fear of failing and being judged
- *We've tried this before. These things never work.*
  The fear of raising hopes and then being disappointed
- *What will our neighbors and ministry partners think if we do this?*
  The fear of incurring a backlash
- *What if we lose the Rogers family and their pledge?*
  The fear of scarcity
- *If we do this, won't some people leave?*
  The fear of disappearing
- *I find their music loud and theologically simple. Let's not dumb things down.*
  The fear of foreign cultures
- *I'd like to see them in leadership, but can we really trust them to do it right? Will they try to take over our church?*
  The fear of letting go of control
- *Wouldn't they be more comfortable with their own people?*
  The fear of facing our own prejudice

If you hear yourself speaking or thinking these statements over time, investigate the story behind the statement. What makes me think that? What experiences or assumptions suggest that this is true? Does this have to be the case? Acknowledge what truth the fear may reveal. Then pause and ask what else is going on, if you are allowing a legitimate concern to take on greater power, cause paralysis or turn your attention from a challenging but faithful course of action. This may very well be the voice of fear.

Holding the Fear

Hearing the fear is one thing. Holding it is something else. Ronald Heifetz, a noted psychiatrist, business expert and professor at Harvard University's Kennedy School of Government, has helped secular institutions to make that transition. He starts by describing change processes as "adaptive work":

> Adaptive work consists of the learning required to address conflicts in the values people hold, or to diminish the gap between the values people stand for and the reality they face. Adaptive work requires a change in values, beliefs, or behavior.[2]

Heifetz then draws a conclusion many pastoral professionals could have guessed: if you are going to lead a community through adaptive work, you have to create a "holding environment" to contain the stress of change.

- *A holding environment isn't just a structure; it is a relationship.* Within the context of this trusting bond, the parties can experience the relaxation, freedom and challenge necessary to continue engaging in change.[3] The holding environment may be the relationship between a politician and his constituency, the coach and her team, a minister or other church leaders and the congregation, or between one friend and another. Certainly, the church body itself may serve as a holding environment for parishioners. Whatever its shape, the holding environment is marked by trust and pre-dictability. People need to be able to trust that the relationship will be there for them, and that it will serve them well.

- *The holding environment doesn't protect people from adaptation.* Neither does it always give them what they want. As Heifetz explains, "the point . . . [is] not to eliminate stress but to regulate and contain stress so that it [does] not overwhelm them."[4] Within this relationship, we can face our fears knowing we will not be ridiculed, exploited or rejected. We can tell the stories of how life used to be, how much we miss it, how everything is swirling and how desperately we want to jump off the merry-go-round. That is the pastoral element.

- *The holding environment facilitates prophetic movement.* So we will be pushed, and we will experience stress, but because of the foundational trust of the holding environment, and because the stress is being introduced at a pace we can bear, we will be able to bend knowing we will not break. When the time is right, we can hear compassionate, persis-tent questions that would have made us balk before, can see images that challenge reality, and can imagine life differently and plot the steps necessary to walk toward that new way of being.

---

2. Ronald Heifetz, *Leadership Without Easy Answers* (Cambridge, MA: Harvard University Press, 1994), 22.

3. Ibid., 104–13.

4. Ibid., 106.

Every leader I spoke with insisted that there is no way to make deep change without this strong commitment to holding people's fears and concerns well. "There is a deeply pastoral dimension to this change," St. Bartholomew's-New York rector Bill Tully told me. "The first year, I wasn't just a CEO. I was a pastor. You take soundings, hold dinners and one-to-ones, listen to people." Meanwhile, Earl Kooperkamp of St. Mary's-West Harlem told me the secret to lasting transformation is pure presence. "If you want change, you have to establish a relationship of trust and love. There are people who disagree with what we're doing here, but I know what's up with them. We know each other. That relationship is what undergirds everything else."

> I once asked to have a different table for the offering. The Altar Guild rep got his knickers all in a knot, stopped talking to me. I said too bad, because I'm still going to talk to you. I rub them, but we still love each other.
>
> CECILY BRODERICK Y GUERRA,
> ST. PHILIP'S-HARLEM

You can't afford not to create and nurture the holding environment. How else will people relax and trust enough to face their fear and risk and grow and walk—together? But how do you create and nurture that holding environment in your own congregation? How does it operate on the ground? These practices will stand you in good stead as you help your community to walk with fear.

Practices for Reckoning with Fear

Practice compassion with your own fears.

Remember: holding fear starts at home. The simple truth is that it is impossible to act as a healer for others if you are hiding from your own fears and haven't learned how to bring compassion to yourself. Be gentle with yourself, and others will sense the graciousness in you. Be unforgiving of your own fear, and others will experience an edge of judgment and impatience in you. So physician, heal thyself. Make it clear to others that you are working with your own fear and vulnerability, perhaps by taking anti-racism or anti-homophobia courses or by sharing stories appropriately in the pulpit or wherever you have voice.

Certain spiritual practices can provide a context for literally sitting with our fears. In *Broken Open: How Difficult Times Can Help Us Grow*, Elizabeth Lesser shares her own toolbox of practices, including prayer, meditation, psychotherapy, storytelling, journaling, painting, exercising, and more.[5] Take your pick. Sit in prayer. Sit in meditation. Sit with pen in hand and

---

5. Elizabeth Lesser, *Broken Open: How Difficult Times Can Help Us Grow* (New York: Villard, 2004).

prepare to tell the truth about your experience. Find a practice and do not be afraid to come back to it again and again.

When we sit gently with fear and see it more clearly, alchemy occurs. We change fear from a silent force that grows in dark corners into a different material altogether, something sad and funny and deeply human. We listen to learn the story of our own fear, and then we can offer up a different one: the story of survival, the story of increased wisdom and strength, the story of new relationships and a closer walk with Christ.

Open the space for honesty and truth-telling.

Fear will find a voice. Will it be a whisper behind a cupped palm, accompanied by a slanted glance and rolling eyes? Or could you shut down those counterproductive, often poisonous backroom conversations by opening up the space for honest, careful reckoning?

If you choose the latter, know that simply speaking about the reality of fear and the need for healing has a powerful effect. Model it from the pulpit.[6] Follow up with Christian formation and community conversations about topics like healing, loss, anti-racism, privilege, the denominational legacy, the changing community, and more—anything that will surface fear. In individual and group sessions like this, invite people to come together in order to give voice to their anxiety and then to explore in a safe space what their fear may be telling them.[7]

Train a team of leaders committed to pastoral care and transformation.

Senior pastor or rector, assistant, lay leader, children's ministry specialist, elder, altar guild member: anyone can take up the vocation of healer and help to initiate and facilitate conversations about fear, hope and gospel-based transformation. It is especially useful to have parish leaders—members of your vestry or church council, the team charged with crafting a fresh vision, the leaders spearheading change or a designated pastoral care team—train to hone their listening and negotiating skills with pastoral care.[8] They should also be equipped with anti-oppression trainings, because they will need to

---

6. See Barbara Lundblad's *Transforming the Stone: Preaching Through Resistance to Change* (Nashville: Abingdon, 2001).

7. For more resources to help facilitate honest conversation in your church, go to Katie Day's *Difficult Conversations: Taking Risks, Acting with Integrity* (Bethesda, MD: Alban Institute, 2001).

8. For pastoral care training, start with Befrienders' Ministries: (phone) (651) 962-5775; (e-mail) befriender@stthomas.edu; (website) www.befrienderministry.org.

understand the way systems of oppression hurt both the oppressed and the oppressor.[9] Though it may be a small group, this pastoral team should reflect the various groups in the congregation, including those who have been marginalized. Everyone in the congregation should be able to approach at least one of these caregivers and leaders with their fears, and know they will be held with respect, compassion and skill.

Bring compassion and wisdom to the resistance.

It is critical that healers learn how to bring both compassion and wisdom to meet fear. To picture those pastoral or prophetic skills in action, it may be helpful to return to just a few of the comments from the "The Sound of Fear" on pages 140–41. How do you respond to a person grappling with the fear of change when it manifests in these familiar ways? First, just listen and offer the gift of your attention and curiosity. Don't jump to debate or change someone's mind. Just listen. Imagine the fear and the story behind it. Feel free to ask the person what that story is. You may also find these insights useful:

Online Extra: Exercises for Meeting Fear with Compassion and Wisdom

- *But I come here to feel good and safe. Is that so wrong?*
  The fear of being uncomfortable in a place that always felt like "home"

  There is nothing wrong with safety and healing, but they should prepare us to go forth and take risks and make disciples in the name of God. And sometimes welcoming others into the church and allowing them to claim it as their home will require us to adjust what has made the space feel like such a home for us.

- *I hope they don't expect us to change our liturgy.*
  The fear of losing a venerable tradition

  Especially for Anglicans, holding onto a particular form of the liturgy is how we hold onto our link to the historic, liturgical tradition. But don't forget that the Anglican tradition began as an effort to create not just a common liturgy but a liturgy of the common people in a language that

---

9. For anti-oppression and multicultural organizational development resources, start with the following:

- *Crossroads Ministry*: www.crossroadsministry.org
- *Seeing the Face of God in Each Other*: www.episcopalchurch.org/ministries/racial-reconciliation/resources/
- *Visions Incorporated*: www.visions-inc.org.
- *Kaleidoscope Institute*: kscopeinstitute.org.
- *Absalom Jones Center for Racial Healing*: www.centerforracialhealing

spoke to their context. It may be that our most faithful, most genuinely Anglican response is to allow the tradition to birth new life in fresh soil.

- *It's not a judgment—they're just not like us.*

The fear of losing a community's cultural, social identity

Of course people are different, and those differences can cause some discomfort. But the amazing grace of church is that it draws together people who would never develop relationships or even acknowledge each other's existence in everyday life. Are there ways that people with different perspectives can enhance our own conversion? Perhaps in the act of letting go of our dominant cultural and social assumptions, we will make room for other ways—and ultimately for God.

- *But shouldn't we study it a little more? We've never done this before.*

The fear of looking ignorant, unprepared or otherwise less than "together"

It's wise to conduct research, do due diligence, sketch various scenarios and assess risk. But if we think these plans will guarantee success, if we believe we can somehow achieve perfection or that God requires it of us, then we're in for sure disappointment. Worse yet, we could end up bogged down or paralyzed just when God is calling us to move.

- *What if we mess it up?*

The fear of failing at something truly significant

Again, our efforts to give our best to God are noble. But when will we learn that our failures teach us as much as any success ever could? Perhaps the goal is not to avoid messing up, but to create a culture where leaders are equipped to make smart decisions, and where members trust each other's wisdom, forgive each other and reflect together when the outcomes don't match the expectations and hopes.

- *What if we lose the Rogers family and their pledge?*

The fear of scarcity *and* the fear of rejection

Anyone's departure feels like a huge loss, especially if that family takes a significant financial contribution with them. It makes us question everything when someone who cared so much about the community walks away. So go ahead and ask the looming question: Are we really on the path to which God has called us? If the answer is no, then continue discerning and don't be afraid to recalibrate. But if the answer is yes, then this is the time to walk in faith. Let's be resourceful, ask remaining members to give more, locate funding outside the congregation. Let's share our story more broadly and boldly, drawing new members who resonate with the gospel-rooted vision we have discerned. Let's trust

> Some of the impetus I have for doing reconciliation work is my memories of what it's like to be marginalized. I listen to people, I hear their anger and pain, and I wonder if there's a hint of their feeling marginalized, too. I try to go to that place of compassion for them.
>
> SARAH DYLAN BREUER,
> EDITOR, THE WITNESS

that the Rogers family may need to find a community that lives into their understanding of the gospel. And let's have faith and pray that, even if some people disagree with our welcoming, they may eventually look back, see our vibrant witness, and learn from it.

These are only examples of how the voice of compassion and wisdom meets the voice of fear. It is empathetic, but not patronizing. It recognizes that there may be a story behind the fear, and it honors the wisdom and truth of that story.

All that said, remember that the wisest course early on may be to say very little, and instead to sit with people while they reckon with their own fear. Bombarding people with reasonable words, however compelling, may just shut down a meaningful conversation and relationship. Stay connected and know that it doesn't have to all happen at once.

Use and share breath and meditation practices.

Lay leader Sarah Dylan Breuer shared these strategies from her Maryland community. "As the director of Christian formation, I'm teaching and leading and encouraging people to be in their own skin," said Breuer, the editor of The Witness magazine and one of the leaders of Gathering the NeXt Generation, the Episcopal group for Generation X leaders. "Breathe. Do it for twenty seconds whenever you get into your car. Notice what you're feeling. Try to instill and nurture the sense that I'm here and it's alright. This practice lays the groundwork for the deep healing and reconciliation that needs to happen, and it's leading us to a place we can return to. When things get tough, they can say, 'Hey, let's go back to that place and then we can keep up the conversation.' It's about having practical tools for reconciliation work."

Be prepared for the backlash.

Once you step out front, be prepared for the backlash. Though you imagine yourself working with the best of intentions ("I'm just trying to help them . . ."), people are certain to get scared, defensive, anxious, and fearful about change, and you will be a convenient target for their anger and confusion. People will call you a troublemaker, declare that you are not truly Anglican or Lutheran or Methodist—insert your tradition as appropriate. Some will accuse you of trying to fix them, and they will stonewall you. Others will get terrified, and they will focus solely on what is right rather than acknowledge the hard work that waits for each of us as we live into the reign of God. You may also fall into the change-leaders' trap and take a patronizing, condescending, arrogant attitude toward your brothers and sisters in Christ. Know that these natural reactions are coming down the pike—yours and theirs. When they do, greet them with the same compassion and wisdom you've learned to bring to your own fears.

Mine for your tradition's resources for dealing with fear.

Generally, change leaders think of the denominational heritage as an albatross around their necks, more likely to inspire fear than to help people to sit gracefully with transformation. Actually, there are resources aplenty in our respective traditions.[10]

Thomas Cranmer bequeathed to Anglicans a tradition of expressing eternal truths in the "common" language. Thanks to Queen Elizabeth's masterful "Elizabethan Settlement" between warring Catholics and Puritans, we have practice stretching our boundaries to include all of God's children, including those with whom we disagree. The Anglican theological heritage is one that combines edginess, humility, and awe, and is convinced of what is essential and generous with the rest. We can trust there is not one of us who holds all the answers, which allows us to do the smartest thing of all: leave room for the Spirit to move in our midst and reveal truth in the Spirit's own time.

If we embodied this tradition at its fullest, and shared it with the church, we might help to ease some of the rigidity about what is truly "Anglican." The same is undoubtedly true for other mainline church folk struggling to meet the fears of traditionalists who might not actually know the breadth of the tradition. Quite often, the wisdom of the ancients can be more liberating than constricting, more hopeful than fearsome.

Return to the dream.

In the end, nothing pulls us through fear to transformation quite like a clear, compelling vision. Remember Fran Kuchar's enlightened advice, gained the hard way at Grace Church in Lawrence, Massachusetts: "Sure, if we come together there will be things we lose. But look at all we gain: a place that's full of people and filled with so much spirit you can touch it."

As our communities reckon with fear, we can hold out the hope and the dream that God has given us. Don't be afraid to ask people: If money were not an issue, if we had not made that mistake ten years ago, if fear were not

---

10. An accessible primer on Anglican theological voices is Richard H. Schmidt's *Glorious Companions: Five Centuries of Anglican Spirituality*. See bibliography for publishing information.

blocking us, what would we hope to be and do? What can you imagine we will lose? What do you imagine we could gain? Is it worth it? What has it cost us, spiritually and emotionally, not to have The Other as a full, engaged member of this community, to be cut off from others in the body of Christ? Dreaming together and forging a common story and common commitment can help a community to neutralize the power of fear. It can fire our steps when we falter. And it can give us reason to listen to our fear and still say "yes" to transformation that is challenging, surprising and, yes, holy.

Online Extra: Bible Studies on Reckoning with Fear and Embracing Change

❋   ❋   ❋

If churches have been slow to embrace radical change, it is usually because they haven't felt strong or wise or daring enough to take risks. Many congregations have been idling in scarcity and survival mode for so long, the thought of change inspires absolute terror. Facing fear of change and fear of The Other simply is not part of our cultural, operational vocabulary.

But no one ever promised us that being the body of Christ would *not* be terrifying. None of the parishes I visited or scholars and leaders I interviewed indicated there would be no pain or terror. The Scriptures certainly don't make that claim. Christ's promise was that we would not be overcome by the spirit of fear, because we would be given the Spirit of power to do the work of God (2 Timothy 1:7). Our challenge is to create communities that know how to sit gracefully with fear *and* to cultivate the spirit of power.

GO DEEPER . . .

- Which of the stories, comments or ideas you just read was the most challenging? Exciting? How do they connect with your own story? What do they inspire you to ask or to do?

- How do these reflections link with your church's story, or the stories of churches you've known?

- Which of the fears listed under "The Sound of Fear" (p. 140–41) sound most familiar to you? Under what circumstances have you or others spoken words like these?

- What are your personal fears around radical welcome? What are your community's fears likely to be?

- Did you notice a practice or suggestion that would help you to bring compassion to your fear or the fear in your community? How might you put it to use?

Where Do We Go from Here . . . Now?

Change is not immediate. First, you literally have to
dance around the edges. But then we broke some
important patterns and now the creativity is flowing.

LUCIE THOMAS, (FORMERLY) ST. PAUL'S-DULUTH

The original edition of *Radical Welcome* included a chapter filled with
insights and practices designed to guide communities setting out on the
road to transformation. After more than fifteen years of further testing, listening, failure, feedback and trying again, I'm grateful to offer wisdom that has
stood the test of time, along with fresh learnings about managing change.

The Practices of a Radically Welcoming Community

So far you've been asked to engage in a lot of internal thinking, sharing, and
discernment. Ultimately, radical welcome is a spiritual practice of extending hospitality and dismantling barriers. It's active and transformative. Here
is a summary of the practices others have taken on as they made their way
toward radical welcome; they're also the attitudes and behaviors you'll need
to cultivate for this renewed way of life.

Practice 1: Get Rooted in the Love of God

How can I love anybody else if I'm unsure of God's love for me? On the
other hand, how powerful would I be, and what risks could I take, if I were
sure of God's love? Recall the words of priest and prophet Henri Nouwen: "I
am convinced that I will truly be able to love the world when I fully believe

that I am loved far beyond its boundaries."[1] Even as you take steps toward radical welcome, be sure you're also building solid practices for members to experience the original, unconditional, radical embrace of Jesus.

Resources

- The Way of Love, a rule of life for following Jesus and growing in love (available at www.episcopalchurch.org/way-of-love)
- Resources for building intentional small group ministries (available at www.episcopalchurch.org)
- Hospitality 101: Inviting, Greeting & Incorporating—handout and audit (available at www.episcopalchurch.org)
- Invite people to experience God's love through worship, prayer, preaching, fellowship, and Bible study.

Practice 2: Know the Neighborhood

If you think welcome starts at your front door, think again. To radically welcome, you have to get to know your wider community—especially the people who are just beyond your doors who wouldn't dare come inside. That starts with information about who is around.

Resources

- Census Data: data.census.gov/cedsci/
- Neighborhood demographics for each Episcopal congregation (available at www.generalconvention.org/research-and-statistics)
- Neighborhood Prayer Walks handout (available at www.episcopalchurch.org/ministries/evangelism/resources)

Practice 3: Identify Who Is "Other" AND Deal with Power

The Other is any group of people who are likely (or would reasonably expect) to experience patterns of historic, systemic oppression and marginalization in your congregation and denomination, especially given your church's dominant race, culture, language, generation, class, sexual orientation, etc. Look around and be honest about what identity groups are your center (groups that hold power—that is, the ability to have authority or influence, and to have their story, culture, and voice shape the congregation) and who is The Other on the margins (groups that tend to be active but not empowered, on the margins, or outside of your church altogether).

---

1. Henri J.M. Nouwen, *The Life of the Beloved: Spiritual Living in a Secular World* (New York: The Crossword Publishing Company, 1992).

Why does this kind of intention matter? You may feel guilty for having no Black members; meanwhile, the majority of people of color in a one-mile radius are actually Brazilian or Cambodian. You may be doing outreach with college students who are miles away, while downstairs in the soup kitchen there are poor, young people yearning to discover they matter to God and to you. Look around and get to know who is actually the neighbor and Other with whom God invites you into relationship.

Why else do we need to get this intentional and specific? Because radical welcome is about dismantling systemic, historic barriers that have disregarded or discounted some groups while privileging others. You can't dismantle and heal those wounds unless you deal with power and consciously name who has it, who doesn't, whose culture shapes the church's story and history, whose culture hasn't . . . and why.

If your welcome is a more general "we welcome everyone" that can't talk about power and privilege, insiders and outsider dynamics, then the systemic barriers are likely to remain. Your welcome remains a statement, not a reality.

Resources

- The Power Grid [available at www.stephaniespellers.com/radicalwelcome]: This handout helps you to understand and map who is at the center and who is other, and introduces deeper questions like these:

  — What barriers/signs of exclusivity is this group likely to encounter in my church and/or denomination?

  — What has my congregation lost because we lack this relationship?

  — What would we gain if we embraced The Other? How might that change me or my congregation?

  — What gifts might we share with The Other?

Practice 4: Do One-to-One Relational Meetings

The hallmark of radical welcome is mutuality, which means sharing and listening equally, and there's no simpler, more effective tool for this practice than One-to-Ones. Community organizers have honed this relational skill: two people meet for a specific amount of time, with the goal of sharing their foundational stories and discovering shared passions and gifts and eventually casting a vision for shared action. It's a different way of engaging our neighbors, and it leads to mutual transformation. You don't need the perfect words or the right programs. Be ready to share what you love, what keeps you up at night, and what God has stirred up for you, *and* be ready to receive the gifts of The Other, which may be different but quite beautiful.

Resources

- One-to-One Relational Meetings (available at www.episcopalchurch.org/ministries/evangelism/resources/)
- Beloved Community StorySharing project and resources (available at www.episcopalchurch.org/storysharing)
- Do One-to-Ones and StorySharing with members of cultural and identity groups who do not shape the story, leadership, and worship of your church. Let them tell you what radical welcome and sharing power feel like to them (instead of assuming you know and setting up programs to welcome them).

  — Have they ever been part of a community that was especially lively, transformative, or full of love?
  — What experiences have they had with your congregation?
  — What have they heard or assumed about you?
  — What would they gain from a new relationship with your congregation?
  — What would they share?
  — What would your congregation need to change in order to signal radical welcome to their group? If they dare to venture inside, what activities, images, messages, music, and events would make it clear that their voices, presence, and power could have a place at the heart of your life together?

Practice 5: Do Your Homework

You can learn a lot in honest conversation with people whose lives are different from yours. You should also do your homework and take responsibility for learning how structures of oppression have played out historically and how they affect your institution's interactions with particular marginalized and oppressed groups.

In addition to books, films, and courses, we could all benefit from anti-oppression trainings and formation offerings that develop critical consciousness regarding systems, power, identity, and oppression (past and present, individual and communal and structural). Create opportunities to help the whole congregation gain cultural competence about The Other's language, history, religious expressions, arts, and style of leadership and engagement.

Resources

- Anti-Racism and Dismantling Racism Trainings list; also includes programs that reckon more generally with oppression and intercultural relations (available at www.episcopalchurch.org/reconciliation)

- Check out the Episcopal Church website (www.episcopalchurch.org)—or whatever faith tradition you call home—and discover resources that support youth and young adult ministries; ethnic ministries, including Latino/Hispanic, Black, Asiamerican, and Indigenous; racial reconciliation, justice, and healing; social justice and advocacy; and domestic poverty engagement.

Practice 6: Build a Change Coalition

If you're a congregational leader, you can build passion by focusing your preaching and Christian formation programs on topics like embracing the stranger, welcoming transformation as a gift from God, and setting the prisoner free (including the prisons that trap privileged people). You can also introduce the idea that church is a community drawn together across boundaries to follow Jesus and grow loving, liberating, life-giving relationship with God, each other, and all of creation (that's straight from the Episcopal description of "The Jesus Movement"—find more at www.episcopal church.org/jesus-movement).

Preaching and solo leadership won't result in lasting change, so build a coalition of people who are committed to the radical welcome vision. It may be the vestry or church council, the welcoming team, or a social justice ministry, but make sure the circle includes people who share passion *and* have the respect and regard of peers. Also engage leaders who identify with the margins, even if they're not active members. Their wisdom will help the whole community to move toward deeper change and help to ease entry for others coming from the margins.

Resources

- Episcopal Church Foundation Vital Teams Program (available at www.episcopalfoundation.org/programs/vital-teams)
- Gil Rendle, *Leading Change in the Congregation: Spiritual and Organizational Tools for Leaders*
- Gil Rendle and Alice Mann, *Holy Conversations: Strategic Planning As a Spiritual Practice for Congregations*
- Eric Law, *Sacred Acts, Holy Change: Faithful Diversity and Practical Transformation*

Practice 7: Strengthen the Holding Environment

Eventually, you'll need to deal honestly and compassionately with your church's fear and resistance. The only way is by nurturing your community's "holding environment"—the set of relationships and rituals that help people to feel safe enough to face change with courage and hope.[2]

How do you do that?

- Provide deep pastoral care to all members, including those who are resistant to change (use the pastoral moment to listen, pray, and prepare people for change).
- Practice open, effective communication, especially across cultural and power divides.
- Offer a wide variety of forums and opportunities for truth-telling, story-telling, and healing throughout the community.

It also helps to identify bridge people (leaders from the center *and* the margins who have the respect of their peer groups) who can help to lead change and nurture mutual relationships. Finally, it's wise to provide regular, reliable opportunities for members to ask questions and offer feedback to key leaders. If you do, remember to follow up, address concerns, and incorporate good ideas.

Resources

- Ronald Heifetz, *Leadership Without Easy Answers*
- Katie Day, *Difficult Conversations*

Practice 8: Get Out There

Where are the people you long to embrace already finding life and community? Go there: to cafés, community centers, markets, daycare centers, the dog park, the soup kitchen, English as a second language programs, music stores, colleges, cultural gatherings. The point is to meet people where they are rather than require that they find their way to you. Enjoy life with them and grow relationship rather than simply advertising for your programs. Eventually, you may share a warm welcome to your community.

It will help if leaders from marginalized groups are shaping this effort and offering insight into appropriate methods and activities. Why? Because you don't know what you don't know. If you have no existing relationships with The Other, cultivate links in the surrounding community—civic, political groups, and broad-based community organizations—in order to increase your cultural competence, visibility, and skill at partnering with The Other. Remember that your goal isn't to acquire more of "them," but to eliminate barriers and share mutual relationship that blesses everyone.

---

2. Ronald Heifetz, *Leadership Without Easy Answers* (Cambridge, MA: Harvard University Press, 1994), 104–13.

Practice 9: Embrace and Be Changed

Over time, with prayer, intention, and a Holy Spirit boost, the gifts, voice, and presence of people from the margins can transform the elements of your congregation's life: mission, identity, ministries, leadership, and worship. Here are some ways to further open the door:

- Establish multiple points of entry to and relationship with your congregation: sponsor relevant community programs and events, offer hospitable space for community groups.
- Start—but don't end—with "diversity" moves: those specific, strategic efforts that increase representation and visibility of underrepresented groups. Be sure to back these new leaders up with extra encouragement, capacity-building, and support, and communicate with the rest of the community about why leadership like this matters in the body of Christ.
- Watch for systemic oppression in your congregation or institution, which may show up as small but debilitating "microaggressions" that ultimately tell The Other they are neither trusted nor wanted.
- Engage in parallel development, that is, nurturing alternative worship and community spaces where the voice of The Other can flourish, *and* create intentional opportunities for the alternative and mainstream to come together and begin to transform the mainstream.
- Nurture collaborative ministries that draw different groups together in order to share leadership and teach each other.
- As your community learns to embrace The Other, try to stretch and make room not only for the "safe" people on the margins, but eventually those whose presence, voice, and power present a real challenge to the dominant culture. Imagine crossing not one but two or more lines: class *and* race (not just Black and Latino educated professionals, but working class and poor people of color), age *and* sexual orientation (not just middle-aged gay men and lesbians, but young and edgy queer folk), etc.

Resources

- "Make Your Church a Center for Blessing" handout (available at www. episcopalchurch.org/ministries/evangelism/resources)

GO DEEPER . . .

- Which of the stories, comments, or ideas that you just read was the most challenging? Exciting? How do they connect with your own story? What do they inspire you to ask or to do?
- How do these reflections link with your church's story, or the stories of churches you've known?
- Have you seen communities striving for greater inclusivity and welcome only to come away bitter and disillusioned? What happened? What planning or approaches would have helped?
- What are the first steps—or the next steps—you would take in your community to nurture radical welcome? With whom might you partner for this work?

PART IV

Community Reflections on Radical Welcome

The Way of Radical Welcome

MARK BOZZUTI-JONES

If, today, you hear these words harden not your hearts

Witness our calling to the principle and foundation of following Christ:

In this body where we welcome—
>we make a way of love, (welcome) lots of love—lots of love (welcome)—
>not an easy discipline (at all).

There's (wide) justice and (broad) compassion and (prodigal) sharing

within (without) the body (different parts, essential parts, all heart really)

and the same gifts (blessings and love) this golden rule of living

spread out to the wider community and the world—golden rule style.
>Nobody (imagine that) gets thrown away or shoved aside (believe that).

Rather, the ones (you, too)
>who might have landed on the scrap heap in the world's economy
>(or the world's culture) are invited to a place at the table within the house
>(welcomed) to the center in Christ's body (seen as becoming Christ's body),
>where they (live) stand, lead, pray (loved and welcomed every day)
>sing and proclaim right alongside the traditional power brokers (live).

What a day of rejoicing that will be?

The ones who've held privilege feel their hearts stretch (burn really),
>grow (ache for justice) and fill (with the blessings of salvation),
>as they discover the joy of offering *and* receiving,
>transforming *and* being transformed (fruits of the Spirit).

There's a lively zing (bling)

as people share the good news of Christ in their own language
(diversity ascending),

and a deep resonance as together they all draw closer
to the brightly burning fire of the living God.

If this vision gives you a charge and a thrill, (might kill you)
even if it scares you but you pray for hope and courage (this you can do)
that's bigger than your fear (walk on water) . . .
then welcome (and welcome another). *Welcome to radical welcome.*

Will she be a lone voice?

Will her voice be unheeded?

Where is the desert from which she cries? Will we eat the locusts,
wild honey, and the bitter herbs of welcoming the radical welcome
that cries in the wilderness?

This, this, this radical welcome done in memory of the One who loved us
to death

This, this, this radical welcome that we remember because God is with us
here in the other, the hungry, the thirsty, the imprisoned, the naked,
the stranger, and the those people who are at our door knocking,
the those people left for dead on the road,
and the those people begging at the door of our churches,
and the those people who are not like us and who do not believe like us

Radical welcome to the enemy, because what is the profit or sense
of welcoming only those who welcome us?

Following the Way of Love stands at the doorway of radical welcome

Embracing God—let God embrace you

Embracing The Other: let the last, least, lost, and lonely embrace you in
their radical welcome

Embracing the Spirit of Transformation:

be careful what you wish for (these days)

If the Spirit embraces you will have to pay the price and take up the cross
of radical welcome

Yes, a radical welcoming we have to do

Let our radical welcome be the dream that Jesus dreamed

Let it be that great strong heart of love

O, let the church be a place where welcome is the air we breathe

O, let the church be the church again

The reign of God that never has been yet

And yet must be—this place of radical welcome that is free

In a world of welcome that is plain to see

A radical welcome is in memory of Me

Yes, a radical welcoming we have to do

Just the worst and best time of the year

For a journey, and such an eternal and essential journey

Radical welcome in the midst of distancing—a difficult time we had of it

But there is no other way. It is the Way

This radical welcome is the Way, the Truth, and the Life . . .

All this is not a long time ago, it is now needed

Over and over again, we have not succeeded. Set this down

This: we shall overcome all resistance to radical welcoming.
      In it we shall find our birth and death

In it we shall not be satisfied with the old dispensation,
      an old clutching of pearls and gods that get in the way

Radical welcoming, we know, we know, we know is the Way . . .

It is all about the radical welcome journey, the mapping of the way,
      the God of welcome, the God of grace, with hearts wide open,
      getting real, facing our fears, and embracing the dream,
      and finding joy in the struggle

Engage God's mission

And hear ye the words of the Sister. She knows and she is Spelling it out
      (as good Spellers do):

"Radical welcome is the spiritual practice that allows us to live into the
      compassionate, just, colorful, boundary-crossing dream of God.
      It's a lot more than a warm welcome at the church door on Sunday
      morning, or a full platter of donuts and flavored coffees in the church
      hall. A radically welcoming community seeks to welcome the voices,
      presence and power of all people—especially those who have been

defined as The Other, pushed to the margins, cast out, silenced and closeted—so they can help to shape the congregation's common life and fulfill the reconciling dream of God. This welcome is not afraid of reckoning with the nitty-gritty roots, the Jesus-level questions about *power* and fear and resurrection and surrender. It has the potential to touch every aspect of congregational life, making room for fresh voices and perspectives to join trusted traditions in shaping the church's mission, identity, worship, ministries and leadership. That's why it's radical."

Walking with Radical Welcome

JENNIFER BASKERVILLE-BURROWS

Stephanie Spellers' work has been my constant companion since the early years of my priesthood. We first met when I was a guest speaker in a class she was taking with the Rev. Dr. Sheryl Kujawa-Holbrook at Episcopal Divinity School in 2001. A few years later, I was on the board of the Episcopal Evangelism Society when we discussed funding the project that would become the book *Radical Welcome*. In my early days as rector of Grace Church in Syracuse, New York, we prepared for the book's publication by working our way through the discussion questions we downloaded from the Church Publishing website. In 2005, once the book was in print, we purchased copies for vestry members and other lay leaders.

Radical Welcome followed me to Chicago in 2012 when I joined Bishop Jeffrey Lee's executive team in the Diocese of Chicago. Workshops based on the book were already in full swing, and I reveled in the opportunity to dive deep with congregations and leaders who were struggling to put some real muscle behind the words "The Episcopal Church welcomes you." Now, nearly ten years later, the opportunity to reflect on this text again, in the midst of the COVID-19 pandemic, has reminded me not only of how much I've "read, marked, and inwardly digested" the wisdom in its pages. but also how much it still has to teach me.

When *Radical Welcome* was first published, I clearly remember the work I needed to do with myself and the people in my parish in Syracuse to get over the title—specifically, the word "radical." Episcopalians seeking to be welcoming, which we believed with all our might we were, did not want to be perceived as radical. But upon reflection and study, we had to admit that it was actually really hard to be as welcoming as Spellers was calling us to be. Looking back, I see that we were struggling with some of the most foundational teachings of our faith.

By defining the kind of welcome we aspired to practice as "radical," Spellers was inviting us to be transformed by the people we hoped would join us, just as Christians are continually being formed into the likeness and mind of Christ. We, on the other hand, were ready to be radically changed by Jesus, but were not so sure about being even minimally changed by anyone who might just show up on the doorsteps of church. Weren't we inviting them to join *us*? And even though being radically welcoming as a numerical growth strategy was debunked in the first chapter of the book . . . well, we were all secretly hoping for just that.

Reading *Radical Welcome* as a congregation all those years ago gave us a common vocabulary to discuss the realities and discomforts that came with our growing openness to being transformed by Jesus and the other. We were able to name the fear and grief that comes with being radically welcoming, but we also learned to look back over the congregation's history to see that being radically welcoming made it what it was—an integrated community of Blacks, Whites, and a few Indigenous folks who came together in the late 1950s as urban renewal destroyed its majority Black, historically Jewish neighborhood. Clearly, Grace Church understood what it meant to welcome those on the margins, but the concept of radical welcome pushed us to bring that legacy into a new era, welcoming people with backgrounds we hadn't before thought of reaching out to or being changed by. As we grew in number, we celebrated the gifts of steadfast members and newcomers alike.

We learned to look for representation in age, gender, race, and class in all aspects of our congregational life, from the acolyte rota to the composition of the vestry. Far from manufacturing diversity that looked good only on the surface, Grace Church took seriously calling people of all kinds into ministries of teaching, serving, and leading. College students served on vestry and directed the choir, mobility-impaired elders led in worship, lay preachers and worship officiants reflected the racial diversity of the parish.

A typical Sunday worship service at Grace might have included hymns from the *Hymnal 1982*, an offertory by the youth choir singing a Kirk Franklin jam, and a saxophone postlude of a Take 6 number performed by the student organ scholar and his visiting family. Every Sunday the beaded cross given by descendants of Deacon David Pendleton Oakerhater, the first Native American deacon in the Episcopal Church, ordained in that very building, adorned the credence table. Our worship was coherent and stunningly beautiful, reflecting as it did the cultures of the people in the pews.

That was almost ten years ago, and I don't want my nostalgia to underplay the disciplined and tenacious work that was required to transform our congregational life and worship. It was incredibly hard and totally worth it to lead a congregation with that kind of dedication to true diversity and commitment to radically welcome.

Ten years on, as the Episcopal Church strengthens its commitment to dismantling systemic racism, and as the world slowly emerges from the COVID-19 global pandemic, I think that we are in the perfect moment to revisit *Radical Welcome*.

In one sense, every moment presents the perfect opportunity, because if radical welcome is the lifelong spiritual practice of seeking to be changed by those we find on the margins, then the right time is always now. The pandemic, however, has taken away any plausible deniability we may have held onto about not knowing or seeing or being proximate to those who are different from us—no matter how we define our particular margin.

In the starkest terms possible, the COVID-19 pandemic has revealed the inequities in our healthcare and education systems and the economic fragility that is the reality for a majority of people in the United States. As congregations ceased worshipping in person, they came face to face with disparities like the lack of access to smartphones and internet connections which, practically overnight, became mandatory for participating in worship, school, and work. Many congregations also came to find that worshipping online made church accessible to people who are physically unable to make it to our church buildings. By rethinking food pantries, meal programs, clinics for the uninsured, and more, they pivoted to meet the exploding needs of the suddenly jobless and underemployed. These have been enormous and sometimes overwhelming tasks, but radical welcome would challenge us also to ask if we are being given an opportunity to reset relationships with those we serve by moving toward mutuality.

As we enter the "new normal" of life after COVID-19, we must ask what radical welcome looks like now. In particular the reflection questions offered in the chapter "Living with Arms Wide Open" are worthy of reflection now: "When have you seen your church relinquish its carefully crafted plans and expectations? What happened? How were you tested? Did you change? How? How did the experience affect your faith?"

For many of us, the new normal will include some version of hybrid church that nurtures Christian community both in person and online. As we embark on that way of worshipping, we need to ask what radical welcome looks like when worship is livestreamed, and formation and fellowship opportunities take place on Zoom. If we can avoid reverting too quickly to old patterns, we can claim the opportunities inherent in these new ways of gathering.

Emerging from the pandemic isn't our only challenge. Our increased awareness of systemic racism and the rise of Christian nationalism present even greater complications for those who truly want to be radical in their welcome. Performative allyship—which Spellers described before the phrase existed—is insufficient, and it is not of the gospel. Radical welcome means that the church doesn't just profess solidarity with people of color or other oppressed groups. Real radical welcome subverts the status quo and instead centers discourse and decision-making on those on the margins.

In a time when the word "Christian" is too often associated solely with a destructive form of White, conservative evangelicalism infused with Christian nationalism, actually doing the work of radical welcome has never been more important. We Episcopalians want to believe that we are different, but if our structures and customs of holding power and resources don't change, and if our congregations continue to be monolithic in race and class, then we can't blame people for not being able to tell us apart.

The beautiful thing about re-revisiting *Radical Welcome* fifteen years on is discovering that it has a timelessness and relevance that we critically need today. In many ways, we are a very different church than when the book was first published. As with many other legacy institutions, we have diminished in number. But we have never been more diverse at the highest levels of churchwide leadership. We are beginning to see the fruit of sustained work to dismantle systemic racism at every level of the church hierarchy. In many quarters of the Episcopal Church, our appetite is growing for deep and vulnerable conversations about who we are and who is truly welcome. On days when I feel impatience at the rate of change, I try to imagine how this beloved church may be transformed fifteen years hence, and I become energized to continue the work. The vision of who we can be, truly reflecting the image of God, is stunningly beautiful and more than worth the effort.

Radical Welcome and Training the Church's Future Leaders

MARK RICHARDSON

In 1999, when I returned to New York City as professor of theology at General Theological Seminary, our eleven-year-old son asked his mother a question in one of those "Jesus moments." On the subway every morning on the way to school, he was disturbed by encounters with homeless strangers asking for money. My wife reminded him, "Whatever you do, don't speak to them. It is not safe to speak with people you don't know on the train." To this advice he replied, "But, Mom, what if one of them is Jesus?"

Brenda and I spent the evening soul-searching. What impression were we leaving about the world we touch daily and the high aspirations of our common prayers (like "Send us out into the world to love and serve You with gladness and singleness of heart")? How quickly children feel the dissonance. They are leaving the church because of it.

Radical welcome is not a sentiment. It is a way of being and acting in the world. Brenda and I had to *do*, not *say*, a response. Brenda and Mark Jr. organized a monthly bake sale to support the homeless shelter based at the seminary, and they sustained this activity through his middle-school years. The church's place is a sign of grace: of thanksgiving for God's unconditional welcome that forms the community of prayer, then sends the community to share this generosity and welcome of God.

If we truly welcome someone, we are willing to be changed by them. They offer a different angle we may not have seen on the infinite variation within the divine life itself, wherein diversity is not simply part of the struggle, not just the cost of love, but its goal, and our desire once we are grasped by this vision.

I imagine the term "radical" to mean that welcome is rooted in this compelling vision of who we are: a vision of God, the source of being who draws *all* things toward their fulfillment within the divine life itself as the outcome of creative love. This is the vision behind "welcome," and as Stephanie Spellers reminds us, it does not anticipate ". . . disappearing, melting into each other."[1] No, nothing is lost, and each aspect of this differentiated unity brings a new angle on the divine image.

Radical welcome is the outcome one would expect and aspire toward if the location of God's saving action is not the church, but *the world*. The church's *being* is in service to and thanksgiving for this unconditional and undiscriminating love of God. If we can capture this image, it changes everything about the way we see those with whom we pray in our church, and the ones we meet for the first time in our neighborhoods.

Radical Welcome and Theological Formation

In a way, everything I've written is prelude to the question I ask myself: "How has radical welcome changed theological education at the Church Divinity School of the Pacific?"

The emphasis in the curriculum of CDSP over the last several years has been a deliberate shift toward preparing leaders to serve the mission of God: strengthening spiritual lives together and building congregations that serve God's mission outside the doors of the church in the neighborhood and world. The assumption of the curriculum is that every area of study—sacred texts, history, theology, practical studies in ministry—ought to serve this aim of *missio Dei*. This can lead us into moments of agitation, not just soul-comfort. When the quest for "realization" is severed from the unfinished work of justice and healing to be done in the world, then we've lost our capacity to be the sacramental sign we are called to be. The assumption in our formation as a community is that worship—eucharistic gathering—is intelligible only when we follow Jesus outside the house of worship into the streets of the village.

One important and required aspect of the CDSP's curriculum in recent years has been our participation in broad-based community organizing led by Industrial Areas Foundation (IAF). Broad-based community organizing

---

1. Stephanie Spellers, *Radical Welcome* (New York: Church Publishing, 2021), 12.

refers to institutions that form an alliance around a common cause, an identified need in a local community, and issues of justice. Although it is institutional, it succeeds on the power and deliberate fostering of personal relationships. I raise the subject of community organizing because I believe it is
grounded—as Spellers concurs—in the same principles as radical welcome.

I have already mentioned the first lesson from this training: relationship building. Community organizing thrives on one-on-one relationships at
the origin of institutional coalition building, engaging people from diverse
backgrounds whom one might not meet otherwise, sharing and listening to
personal stories to discover what matters for each person in the conversation. The method is successful because each speaks within their own voice,
not on behalf of an idea.

As wise figures have stated, story-sharing is the shortest distance
between two lives. I suspect it is because stories express the heart—the
longings, desires, and struggles. Indeed, one of the resurrected Jesus' first
acts is to ask his road companions to tell their stories about what has happened to them. This community organizing process of one-on-one conversations is a first act in building trust and mutual accountability, and it is
the bedrock of successful alliance for achieving a common good. And what
could be more welcoming than to invite one another to tell our stories?

Second, organizing is about *power*—the awakening of the capacity to
act in those who have been either invisible to, or the objects of, the power
of others. I think of my privileges, so often unacknowledged. How rarely
I question the range of agency or freedom I have as an anonymous individual in the streets of a city, or as a professional with a particular standing.
Community organizing and radical welcome are precisely about inviting and
encouraging the power in those who have never been welcomed to claim it.

If we truly mean this beyond gesture, then we open ourselves to being
changed as this new agency meets our own. To hold power *with* others,
instead of power *over* others, will change us. Like waves that sometimes
converge and sometimes run interference patterns, the interference can
break up old patterns, existing habits of action and understanding, to bring
about the unexpected. If our aim is not to incorporate or assimilate others
into a going system, but rather to invite a wider embrace of agency into the
building of new regimes of order, then we have the groundwork for enjoying
the beauty of diversity. This is the grit and traction of welcome: the sometimes jarring effect of *"power with."*

Third, the realism of community organizing is that it contains moments
of agitation, the grind and messiness of moving a complex mix of institutions
toward an action that expresses common interests, the hard work of endless
meetings, and the occasional failed effort to meet the goals of an action.

Community organizing is not easy work, I suspect, because it is about creating practices that break up habits of ease for some in the grids of public life, breaking up policies that have hurt people, and rebuilding toward manageable (not perfect) solutions. Are there messy and exhausting phases of building up the spiritual practices of welcome? Yes, I think so. I suspect that if we are honest, then we will recognize that welcome must acknowledge the agitation leading to change in us. One measure of welcome is when real values and real needs in the places we live are being addressed and we are willing to undergo the labors of getting there.

I remember a wet and cold night in January several years ago when a CDSP class was preparing to participate in an organizing event in Marin County's San Rafael. Community organizers in the area had gathered various constituencies around an action to create change in police treatment of seasonal workers living in the area, and problems of housing associated with these and other lower-income residents. The mayor would be represented, along with police and fire departments and housing officials, all to address gathered constituents who represented a broad range of organizations in alliance. Speakers also included victims who had turned themselves into actors that night by standing up.

But this was not an ordinary January evening in the Bay Area. It began in a deluge of rain quite unlike anything I'd seen. As I drove across the Richmond–San Raphael Bridge in a car filled with students, I thought, "This is going to be a bust. No one's going to show up." As we approached the location for the gathering, the water was rushing down the street overflowing the curb onto the sidewalk. "Who will come out in this kind of weather? And the few who do will be sitting drenched and cold in this school auditorium wishing they were home and dry."

I was so surprised and wrong. The crowd of people began to build, a rising buzz of conversation, and when it was time to start, we were well beyond seating capacity. The energy in the room had a quality of expectation around gatherings of mutual support. Like a marketplace, this was the diversity of the city in a concentrated time and place one rarely experiences—wealthy, modest labor class residents, migrant workers, nuns and priests, city officials, children, and grandparents. This was a room of eye-to-eye, voice-to-voice contact.

How did this happen? What our students witnessed was a visible effect, but only a snapshot in time, of many hours of relationship building—one-on-one conversations which are the building blocks of community organizing. This, and small house meetings, are the unseen foundation of building trust and mutual accountability, all before such evening events take place. And, most important, the public event was a visible sign of invited empowerment—the capacity to act—in one another. Our students were learning a new angle on how to build relationships with one's neighbor and encounter the stranger. They witnessed disciplined and organized relationship building at work toward achieving a common good. When radical welcome is in practice, I suspect this is in the background.

We went home that evening tired and soggy, ready for bed. But more important we went home exhilarated by the short conversations with people sitting or standing next to us from every walk of life, from the racial mix of urban America, and from conversations through smiles and a nod as our only common language. The next day would not be the same as the days before. Not because of wins or losses in the political battlefield, but because we had placed ourselves in the way of the evidence of a still more vast and gracious embrace of God. And *we* had been welcomed into it.

The Defining Core of the Church

In *Radical Welcome*, Spellers asks: "What kinds of activities and relationships reflect the radically welcoming dream of God? . . . How is God calling you to recast leadership and to expand your notion of who is truly worthy of exercising power?"[2] My response is that the training and shaping of new habits (such as relationship building and the give-and-take that goes with it) and actions (shared power or agency)—what many of us have experienced most profoundly in community organizing—all support the move from assimilation to the incarnation of God's diverse family, where all of us can be whole persons. A further premise is that *coalition in action* toward a common goal for our communities can be an ideal way of breaking barriers with those we do not know in our neighborhoods. It is a starting point of shared power that can take us to new places.

One CDSP student, Luis Ottley, also the headmaster of a school, had low expectations coming into this kind of training, figuring that as a student of color he would be the designated "other." He was accustomed to the church's ingrained habits of turning both insiders and outsiders into "other." But he came to see the goals and practices of organizing as hand-in-glove with what the church says about itself in its covenants, a way of action that might give us hope. He concluded that ". . . broad-based community organizing is a fundamental vocation for all Christian living. . . ." What did he mean? In effect, he echoed Spellers, who points out: These practices turn us toward a posture of ". . . embracing and being changed by the gifts, presence, voices, and power of The Other."[3] Such tools and goals help

---

2. Ibid., 91.

3. Ibid., 6.

us to bring fresh attention to the baptismal covenant, grounded in God's welcome. Love of neighbor, striving for justice and peace, respecting the dignity of every human being: these are not add-ons to the church's being; they are the defining core.

Whether headmasters or leaders of congregations or institutions, we have found that deepening this art of conversation, story-sharing/story-listening, and power sharing can be the path for discovering and drawing out lay leadership teams in our churches.

Often, students preparing for ministry are predisposed to think of power as a matter of dominance or possessing control and influence over others. When power is seen as control, it feels like a zero-sum engagement: some will have it, others will not—precisely the terms of assimilation. But if power is a neutral term with open possibility—the power to act—then we can imagine power *with* the other, or acting *with* the other, and not *over* the other. This itself will require us to change, but not to lose our own agency. True relationship is interdependence, not control. Yet, this is enough to stimulate, even agitate, as we open ourselves to changing with others. This is where one-on-one relationships become the key; we welcome the other to tell their personal story, to listen to their desires and struggles, even as we share our own. Dedicating time for this is the foundation of meeting the whole self of the other, and being changed by them.

The tough part will surely be in the details. Spellers reminds us of the pull of habit, particularly the long historic traditions, for example, in liturgical clothing, language, and actions, that anchor Episcopal life and worship in comforts of the familiar. Like a mantra, the very utterance of the prayers, quite apart from their substance, has spiritual affect. Yet even those of us who feel this also feel the exhilaration of a new sound, a new voice and cadence. This seems analogous to various facets of all historic forms of life on the one hand, and fresh new possibilities and new forms on the other. We will all have a different point to mark "what is essential and cannot change" and what will stretch us out of the familiar and lead us into transformation and a closer walk with Jesus. This will take us back over and over to ask: What is so fundamental to our *true* identity that it cannot change? Paradoxically it may be the vision of the God of love at work in us to convert us and lead us beyond our own best ideas into God's future. Our faith itself, in other words, is about letting go, truth telling, conversion, and thus, openness to change.

Most students and faculty at CDSP would tell you that this is a struggle and it is ongoing work for our community. We are conscious of and eager to discover and change the forces of assimilation affecting those who enter our community year after year. But we are also aware of the power of assimilation lingering in patterns of chapel worship, classroom pedagogies, standards of evaluation, forms of community gathering. These are the not-so-visible forces of institutional *stasis*, and it's not always easy to examine them. Like the imaginary fish in the pond that asks where the water is, we are unaware of how the familiar to the insider may be anywhere between unfamiliar and alienating for the new person coming in.

We have learned that if you are preparing to be radically welcoming, then brace yourself. Striving toward this goal must be constant and vigilant. Learning to invite the agency of the other, opening to listen and to share, and being willing to enter the sometimes abrasiveness of change, is not for the faint of heart. But it is, as Ottley states, a fundamental vocation for all Christian living, and we enter it because we expect it to lead to our deepest joy.

A Dream
and a Church
Big Enough for God

Michael B. Curry

Thy kingdom come
Thy will be done
On earth
As it is in heaven

Jesus of Nazareth

There's plenty good room
Plenty good room
Plenty good room in my Father's kingdom

Negro Spiritual

A number of years ago at a preaching conference, one of the present-
ers told a story of an unlettered old black preacher who had been
invited to speak at one of the historically black colleges near the end of
the nineteenth century. After the baccalaureate service he had an intense
exchange with a student.

"So what are your plans for the future?" the old preacher asked.
"Well, I would like to practice law, so I plan to go to law school," the graduate
answered.
"What then?" the old preacher asked.

"Well, I'll take the bar exam.
"What then?"
"Well, I hope to begin to practice."
"What then?"
"I don't know, I guess I'll get married."
"What then?"
"Well, I guess we'll have some kids."
"What then?"
"We'll raise them until they go off to start their own lives."
"What then?"
"I hope my wife and I will grow old together."
"What then?"
"I don't know, I guess we'll retire and enjoy retirement."
"What then?"
"What else is there?"

Then the old preacher said, "Well, my young friend, you've got some good ideas, but your plans are too small. They only concern you and yours. Your plans must be wide enough to include others and high enough to be embraced by God. Then you will live a life that matters."

The Church Today

I can almost hear the old preacher's wisdom speaking anew to those of us who are in church today. When news reports of mainline church decline are reported, or even the general decline in organized religion, there is so often hand-wringing, accusing, and sadness. To be sure, when a local church closes, there is a real loss and appropriate grief. A local church is a sacred place of cherished memories in which our lives have been touched by God and human community from birth to death, in times of sickness and in health. Life has been lived there, and we grieve when it is no more.

But much of the hand-wringing is often more about institutional decline, our loss of place and influence in society, our decline in market share and number-one status, and the overall end of Christendom. When that is the case, the old preacher's wisdom is for us. "You've got some good ideas, but your plans are too small." In fact, I would go a step further and borrow from the title of J.B. Philips' book and say, *Your God Is Too Small*.

As someone who is an unapologetic follower of Jesus in the community called church, I am aware that our plans and indeed our God can easily become too small. God gets reduced to the manageable, the convenient, the easily understandable, sometimes the manipulatable.

But God is always as Paul Tillich once said, "the God above God." The God of the Bible is the one of whom the prophet Isaiah speaks:

> Seek the LORD while he may be found,
> call upon him while he is near;
> let the wicked forsake their way,
> and the unrighteous their thoughts;
> let them return to the LORD, that he may have mercy on them,
> and to our God, for he will abundantly pardon.
> For my thoughts are not your thoughts,
> nor are your ways my ways, says the LORD.
> For as the heavens are higher than the earth,
> so are my ways higher than your ways
> and my thoughts than your thoughts. (Isaiah 55:6–9)

A small God yields small plans, timid efforts, and narrow perspectives. The story of Jonah in the Hebrew Scriptures is a perfect illustration of this. God tells Jonah to go and declare his word to the people of Nineveh. Jonah doesn't want to do it, so he runs away where he thinks God can't find him. He boards a ship to sail beyond God's reach . . . or so he thinks. He ends up cast overboard, swallowed by a great fish, spit up on land, where he eventually gives in and goes to Nineveh.

While there are many messages in the story, one is inescapable: Jonah had a little God. It was a God of his tribe. And this little God led to little plans. Jonah would preach only to his tribe and his people, not others. But Jonah discovered the God whose ways and thoughts are so much higher than ours. He stumbled into what my grandma called "great God Almighty."

He encountered the God who is, as Anselm of Canterbury once said, that of which nothing greater can be thought. The God of whom African slaves in antebellum America once sang, the God who is:

> So high, you can't get over him.
> So low you can't get under him.
> So wide you can't get around him.
> You must come in by the blood of the Lamb.

And that God has a great and sublime plan and purpose for all of creation and all of humanity.

The Jesus Movement

The wisdom of the old preacher has profound and deep implications for those of us who are followers of Jesus and his way of love in the context and community of the church. One of the great temptations of organized religion is to shrink the great mission of God into the perpetuation of the institution and maintenance of the machinery of religion, at the expense of its original inspiration and reason for being. Instead of following Jesus and his way of love to live out God's great mission for God's world, mission is narrowed to the church's mission, which easily gets reduced to institutional preservation and narrow self-interests.

As South African theologian Albert Nolan taught us, "Jesus didn't start an organization, he inspired a movement." It was a movement of those who became part of a community seeking a life centered on Jesus. Energized and guided by the Spirit that energized and guided him, they actually sought to live his teachings, to emulate his example, and to walk his way of love as their way of life.

This does not mean that the Jesus Movement is anti-organizational or anti-institutional. Obviously, any movement needs organization. To be sure, institutions can serve the movement and the cause. But when institution or organization takes precedence over the movement of Jesus and his way of love, then the warning of the old preacher is a prophetic word to the church: "Your plans are too small," and more starkly, "Your God is too small." And ultimately a small God is not God at all, but something masquerading as God. And that is what the Ten Commandments call a graven image and an idol.

The temptation and danger of idolatry is always with us. Anything or anyone becomes an idol when placed in God's stead. Whether family, race, or clan, religion, nation or institution, if it takes the place that only God can and should hold, it has become an idol, a false god.

When religion gets too small, it narrows and becomes self-centered, tribalistic, nationalistic—just another self-serving, self-interest group. That's when alliances between White supremacy and Christianity create justifications for human slavery. That's when religion gets co-opted by cultural, political, racial, ethnic, economic, nationalistic, nativistic, individual self-interest and becomes an instrument of oppression, injustice, hatred, bigotry, and manifold forms of anyone's supremacy over anyone else. And when that happens, religion can provide ideological cover and rationalization for all sorts of evils against God's creation and against other children of God created in God's image and likeness and "endowed by their Creator with certain unalienable rights."

The old preacher was right: "You've got some good ideas, but your plans are too small. They only concern you and yours. Your plans must be wide enough to include others and high enough to be embraced by God. Then you will live a life that matters."

The Dream of God

In great part because of this book and Canon Spellers' work in the church, the phrase "radical welcome" has become more and more well known. It would be easy, though, for the idea of radical welcome to be narrowed into helping our churches and faith communities to become more welcoming to visitors. Don't misunderstand me, that is very important. In fact, practicing hospitality in church can be a way of practicing to be a presence of the radical welcome and hospitality of Jesus in the world. When someone comes through the doors of a church, they ought to be welcomed with our outstretched arms, likened unto the outstretched arms of Jesus on the cross. That's important.

But remember the wisdom of the preacher. We may like the idea of radical welcome, but then our plans get too small. Our concerns are only for ourselves, when they could be widened to embrace others and high enough to connect with God's own plan.

I was profoundly struck years ago when I first read Canon Spellers' book to realize that the message of the church as a community embodying radical welcome is meant to be a witness of God's dream and God's sublime intention for the entire human community and all of God's creation. I want to underscore her wisdom and how important that really is.

Actually I should've known from the first conversation I ever had with Stephanie many years ago. I was a relatively new bishop. I had been invited by the then bishops of Massachusetts to speak at the convention of the diocese. At some point during the proceedings, there was a break. A young priest came up and introduced herself to me. It was Stephanie Spellers. While I don't remember everything we discussed, I do remember we talked about the late Verna Dozier and her understanding of the dream of God.

Dozier spoke often about the God who the Bible says "is love." When God first said, "Let there be . . . ," God (who is love) clearly had something in mind. That something is what Verna named "the dream of God": God's sublime plan, purpose, and intention in the creation of the world and of God's human children.

Josiah Royce, Howard Thurman, and Martin Luther King Jr. spoke of this dream as "the beloved community." Thich Nhat Hahn, whom Dr.

King nominated for the Nobel Peace Prize, has enlarged on this vision of the beloved community to include not just humanity and nations, but all of God's creation. The realization of beloved community in which selfishness is overcome by the way of unselfish, sacrificial love, is clearly a fulfillment of the dream of God, what the God who is love has had in mind since the beginning.

The Bible points to this in the mountaintop vision of Isaiah, in which the wolf will lie down with the lamb, for there is no hurt or harm on God's holy mountain (11:6–9). It is elsewhere in Isaiah and again in Revelation where the end of all things is seen as a new heaven and a new earth (Isaiah 65:17; Revelation 21:1). God's dream of the beloved community is at the heart of what Jesus was referencing when he spoke of the kingdom or the reign of God.

It was that kingdom of God over and against the kingdoms of this world and the self—that kingdom is at the heart of the dream of God and the life and teachings of Jesus. It is solemnly invoked when Jesus teaches his followers to pray with their lips, and with their feet, as Frederick Douglas once said of the prayer:

> Thy kingdom come
> Thy will be done
> On earth as it is in heaven.

For Jesus seeking this kingdom is the key to life. That is why he reassured his disciples in this way:

> Therefore do not worry, saying, "What will we eat?" or "What will we drink?" or "What will we wear?" For it is the Gentiles who strive for all these things; and indeed your heavenly Father knows that you need all these things. But strive first for the kingdom of God and his righteousness, and all these things will be given to you as well. (Matthew 6:31–33)

In words of both warning and witness, Verna Dozier spoke of this type of faith as "kingdom of God thinking," something that resonates for Canon Spellers and for me. As Dozier wrote:

> Faith implies risk. The faith view of reality is frightening in its openness, so institutions are always trying to control reality with doctrines and laws and creeds. Kingdom of God thinking calls us to risk. We always see through a glass darkly, and that is what faith is about. I will live by the best I can discern today. Tomorrow I may find out I was wrong. Since I do not live by being right, I am not destroyed by being wrong. The God revealed in Jesus, whom I call the Christ, is a God whose forgiveness goes ahead of

me, and whose love sustains me and the whole created world. That God bursts all the definition of our small minds, all the limitations of our tired efforts, all the boundaries of our institutions.[1]

Faith such as this does not yield the plans of the small-minded, or trust in a tiny God of our own devising. Faith such as this is real faith in the real God who the Bible says is love.

Our commitment to be not just a welcoming church, but a radically welcoming people, is not based on caving in to a social theory or capitulation to the ways of the culture, but on our commitment to follow the way of Jesus, whose outstretched arms on the cross are a sign of the very love of God reaching out to us all, until God's dream of the beloved community is realized. This high calling will yield a life and a church that are, as the old preacher said, "wide enough to include others and high enough to be embraced by God."

---

1. Verna Dozier, *The Dream of God: A Call to Return* (2006; New York: Seabury Books, 2021), 15.

Conclusion: The Journey Continues

I don't know that we're doing enough to hold out the joy, the vision of what it could all look like. When I talk about change, I see the joy. So how do you communicate that? How do you communicate the value of looking under that rock, behind that door, tapping into Jesus' excitement at walking among the people your culture says you shouldn't be with?

THE REVEREND CANON STEFANI SCHATZ-DUGGAN (OF BLESSED MEMORY), CANON TO THE ORDINARY, DIOCESE OF CALIFORNIA

Early in my radical welcome journey, I stayed at the home of Stefani Schatz-Duggan. I first made her acquaintance when she mentored me and other seminarians at our alma mater, Episcopal Divinity School. But I really got to know her in 2004, while she was leading and loving God's people as a priest in Southern California. She laughed, ate, surrounded us with color, and called us to account. Throughout her career, she prodded and slammed against the stained-glass ceiling that separated women from power, but she did it with such generosity of spirit and joy that you didn't realize the strength of her impact. Later, when she became the first female Canon to the Ordinary in the Diocese of California, I remember thinking, "If this church can make room for someone as honest, wise, wild, generous, and fabulous as Stefani, we're going to be alright."

Stefani died in 2017, much too young. I often look at her words above—a quote I used to open the original concluding chapter of *Radical Welcome*—when I need to get back in touch with why we do what we do. It is only right to invoke her memory and wisdom as I conclude this new edition.

Teachers like Stefani have asked me hard questions and pointed me toward life-altering insights. What wisdom for the road would I retrieve from that first edition? What have we learned over these fifteen years? What's on the horizon?

Does Anyone Feel Welcome?

In workshop after workshop, conference after conference, I've been shocked by how many people of all kinds report they don't feel welcome in church. Radical welcome may emphasize embracing The Other who has been historically, systemically marginalized and exploited for the benefit of the privileged. And yet, if you listen to members of the dominant culture, you often hear a heartbreaking sense of alienation and loneliness. Try telling these folks they're the insiders holding power at the center. It's a hard sell.

On one hand, domination systems survive and regenerate through a sophisticated game of hide and seek. Powerful people often don't realize they're exercising power or privilege; they just see themselves living their individual lives. If you name the structural racism, sexism, elitism, heterosexism, and other oppressive hierarchies at work all around, lots of privileged people resist. "What do you mean, I have privilege?" "I earned this position, and my gender and race had nothing to do with it." "My church is a warm and welcoming place. If people of color or poor people or young people don't attend, it's not because of anything we're saying or doing." This non-seeing serves and soothes the privileged conscience; it also prevents them from asking thorny questions that might threaten the system.

But that's only one reason why people with dominant culture privilege may vehemently deny they're included. Another reason? Because they genuinely don't feel welcome.

One of the first exercises in any radical welcome workshop is an invitation to share in pairs around this question: "Recall a moment when you felt welcomed, fully received, and beloved as part of a church." Some really get it, but some start to squirm. Others report that they don't feel welcomed, certainly no more welcomed than anyone else, and they resent the assumption that they do.

After a few years, I began to pair that exercise with a new one: a meditation on the love of God. A volunteer reads the story of Jesus' baptism in the Jordan, when the Spirit alights on him, and a voice from heaven declares: "You are my beloved; with you I am well pleased" (Luke 3:22 and Mark

1:11). I remind folks that God declared Jesus beloved before he performed one miracle or spoke much in the way of prophecy. God was simply stating what was true from the beginning—that Jesus is beloved—and we all start with the same blessing.

Next I invite participants to breathe in and breathe out. On the in-breath, they imagine God saying, "You are my child." On the out-breath, they hear: "With you I am well pleased." After a few rounds, tears start to leak from their eyes. Soft smiles emerge. Shoulders relax. People need to know they are loved by God. Having rooted ourselves in that original blessing, we can draw from a well of abundant love as we practice radical welcome.

I would never say systems of privilege and exclusion are not real. They endanger and shatter the lives of people in every nondominant group, and they prevent Christian communities living into the fullness of the gospel. At the same time, a lot of people who've spent their lives at church and received every kind of privilege don't know themselves as fundamentally beloved by God. They're still waiting for the welcome that eliminates their bone-deep experience of loneliness and rejection. A radically welcoming ministry will work to build a welcoming, loving culture for everyone, insider and outsider, margin and center.

Whose Vision Is It?

Once upon a time, the rector at St. Bartholomew's in Atlanta tried to plant a new Hispanic ministry. An announcement was made to parishioners. Leaders were given the opportunity to take Spanish lessons. They did lots of advance work, including some in the Latino community. Then they opened the doors. The ministry eventually flopped, largely for lack of real relationships and because the people of St. Bartholomew's had yet to claim the vision as their own.

It was the right thing to do for perhaps the right reasons. It was the decidedly wrong way. "When it comes to welcoming, there has to be ownership," their rector, Mac Thigpen, told me at the time. "If you haven't built the support and understanding, it won't work."

Congregational vision and new directions should certainly be shaped by the rector or pastor and the core elected leadership—that's what leading means. But if the rest of the people have no stake, no voice, no part in crafting that vision, they aren't likely to stay the rough course ahead. It takes time, but discerning God's dream for your community *as* a community is definitely time well spent. (Note: if you're reading this book on your own, please invite others to join you before launching into planning and implementation.)

Some people will balk or call this "over-processing." Shouldn't change happen organically, on the ground? Is all this talk just a stall tactic preventing you from getting down to the "real" work? No and no. It is empowering and enlightening to find appropriate ways of inviting the congregation to discern and voice their hope and claim a vision together—from the newcomers to the veterans who've been sitting in the same pew for fifty years. You don't have to make decisions as a one-hundred-person committee. You don't have to wait for one-hundred percent buy-in before moving ahead. But listen to each other, to the hopes and passions that fuel your community, and then plan wisely. This is the ground in which the seeds of radical welcome will either grow or die.

Here's the bonus: if—or when—complacency or defensiveness kicks in ("Why are you trying to change us? Is something wrong?"), you'll be able to remind people that the community discerned this vision together. Recall the Holy One's invitation in the Book of Isaiah: "See, I am about to do a new thing; . . . do you not perceive it?" We need time and space together to perceive the new thing God is doing among us.

Are You Going to Die in This Ditch?

We also need to be realistic about our resources. It would be wonderful to launch full steam ahead into ten different noble causes, but that's a recipe for burnout and disaster. Instead, assess your human, organizational, and financial resources, and then pace yourself. You need not take on the transformation of every element of the institution—the mission, identity, liturgy, leadership, and ministries—in a single, highly disruptive charge.

Especially if a particular project appears combustible or sensitive, pray and plan well before you barrel in and lose the goodwill and momentum you've hopefully built up. For instance, if you are introducing a Spanish-language service at noon, then keep the beloved 10 a.m. Morning Prayer worship stable. Smart pacing is not an admission of weakness or lack of commitment. It is just the wise thing to do. Take it from *Leading Congregational Change*: "All congregations have resource constraints that cause them to defer other possible actions until later in the process. The ongoing transformation process should include periodic reviews to establish new priorities and implementation plans."[1]

You will also find that, while a particular shift does not represent total alignment with your mission and dream, it could be an important

---

1. Jim Herrington, Mike Bonem, and James H. Furr. *Leading Congregational Change: A Practical Guide for the Transformational Journey* (Hoboken, NJ: Jossey-Bass, 2000), 153.

intermediate step that draws your community closer to the dream of God. In Duluth, Minnesota, members at St. Paul's knew building community relationships and hosting social service programs was not the same as welcoming new voices into the worship, ministry, and leadership of the congregation. But they needed to take that initial step in order to literally open the doors of the church, create space for new relationship, and encourage neighbors to finally claim the "fortress" church as their own.

Congregations aren't simply systems; they are human communities that love, fear, and hope. As urgent as the work may seem—and it is!—please honor the need for stability even as you support transformation. Janet Walton frames the issue well, saying, "Change is inevitable. But it does not mean eliminating all that is familiar, all well-loved language for God, all scripture texts, all typical forms of preaching. . . . It does require examining them and giving up whatever hurts, hides or dishonors."[2] As a congregation, you can discern what most hurts or holds you back, as well as what would be most transforming, lifegiving, and manageable over the long term.

What Comes After Radical Welcome?

For a couple of generations, faith traditions like mine have rightly focused on inclusion and welcome. At times, we've stretched to radical welcome and sought to incorporate, honor and be changed by groups whose voices, cultures, and leadership the church hasn't historically embraced.

I believe in that ministry. I've also been struck by the limits of welcome. Even when church folks go to learn and build relationship with groups on the margins or outside our orbit entirely, the motion remains centripetal: we send word *out there* that we welcome people to *come in* to the church to share life with us.

This is not to say radical welcome is not costly. It destabilizes our understanding and experience of church. It moves you places you would not choose to go. You cannot expect new people and emerging cultures to worship and behave on your group's terms. Rather, groups on the margins begin to share freely what they love and what they know, and use those gifts to reform the congregation and its ministries by your side.

But we're still talking about reforming the life of the congregation or ministry. Is there more? In my reflection and prayer, one word has risen time and again: solidarity. Solidarity does not replace radical welcome, but the two complement each another. Where welcome tends to direct the energy

---

2. Janet Walton, *Feminist Liturgy,* as quoted in Barbara Lundblad, *Transforming the Stone: Preaching Through Resistance to Change* (Nashville: Abingdon Press, 2001), 74.

inside, solidarity sends you out to join what God is working out among different groups and situations, and keeps you out there to enact something holy together. Radical welcome wonders how to share power and life within the church or institution. Solidarity wonders how to realign core elements of my life and the life of my church so that we become a community that follows Jesus wherever he leads.

David Swanson has arrived at a similar conclusion, a journey he details in *Rediscipling the White Church*. According to Swanson, most majority White churches reckon with segregation and racism by seeking inclusion and diversity, as if the core problem is our separation from each other. He warns they've performed a critical misdiagnosis:

> The problem of racism—the actual racial situation in our faith communities—is not separateness itself. And togetherness is certainly no solution. . . . While welcoming people of color into our congregations or ministries would scratch our relational itch, the underlying factors related to our segregation remain unaddressed.[3]

On this point Swanson and I are in sync: getting everyone into one church together, even with attention to power and mutuality, won't bring about beloved community. For that, those at the center must reorient themselves and move into relationship with Jesus who walks so often among the margins and suffering peoples. That's where solidarity comes in.

What is solidarity? It is what love alive looks like. I define it this way in *The Church Cracked Open*:

> Solidarity is love crossing the borders drawn by self-centrism, in order to enter into the situation of the other, for the purpose of mutual relationship and struggle that heals us all and enacts God's beloved community.
>
> Solidarity is the voice that finally comprehends: "You are not the same as me, but part of you lives in me. Your freedom and mine were always inextricably entwined. Now I see it, and because of what I see, I choose to live differently. I will go there, with you, for your sake and for my own.[4]

Solidarity pushes radical welcome to become even more radical. It says, "Don't just sing our songs or enter our neighborhoods. Learn our stories. Walk humbly in our spaces. Divest yourselves of privilege and then sacrifice for the sake of our flourishing. Allow our living and loving to become

---

3. David Swanson, *Rediscipling the White Church: From Cheap Diversity to True Solidarity* (Downers Grove, IL: InterVarsity Press, 2020), 38.

4. Stephanie Spellers, *The Church Cracked Open: Disruption, Decline, and New Hope for Beloved Community* (New York: Church Publishing, 2021), 107.

intertwined with your own." Can we radically welcome and then learn to give our life away for the sake of The Other? If we do, we'll look a little less like church as we've known it . . . and a little more like Jesus.

Is Radical Welcome Worth the Trouble?

The risk is real, but there is so much joy in becoming God's radically welcoming people. When we engage in this practice as communities, we are engaged in knitting together the very body of Christ and abiding more closely in him. And Jesus has promised that, the more deeply we abide in him, the more complete our joy will be. That promise is not a future phenomenon. His joy is available to us, and radical welcome opens us to receive that blessing now.

It's true, no one will get everything they want. When it comes to welcoming change and newness, especially new people, cultures, and traditions, we all need to work hard to relinquish our privilege as people who bear racial, ethnic, linguistic, heterosexual, economic, body-type, clerical status (and on and on) privilege. We may need to let go of the definition of church as the place that feels like family or home. We may need to name and give up our desire to be part of a club where we know everyone, sit in the family pew by ourselves, and enjoy singing all the songs and speaking all the words by heart.

There's no need to swap the entire classical choral canon wholesale for gospel or contemporary music. But can we ask questions about who decided what that canon would be? Can we reshape the canon to make faithful room for each other's gifts, voices, and images? Can we grow to trust each other's skills for leadership? Can we allow our identities to be converted by the encounter with The Other? Can we partner for ministry as equally beloved but differently gifted children of God? Can we make intentional, systemic efforts to open our communities in these ways, knowing that transformation rarely comes from one-shot, one-season programs? And can we do all these things trusting that Jesus will show up to love and beckon us deeper into this radical call?

Even if Jesus is beckoning, change—especially "radical" change—is hard. Under the best of circumstances, God may want to place a blessing in your palm, but first you have to open your hand and turn over something old and comforting in order to receive it. In the face of all that loss, I can't help but recall Jesus' warning that we may need to lose our life, but only so that we will find it.

If that is true, then maybe it is meet and right to strip away some common stereotypes hovering over the church. Are we the gathering of God's radically open, radically loving, radically welcoming people? Then we should make it abundantly clear that we are the least stiff, least unforgiving, least crusty, least homogenous, least fearful, least judgmental people in the world. If our public personae says otherwise, then it's time to change.

There must continue to be room in the church's mission for the members' comfort and healing. We cannot heal the world unless we are simultaneously experiencing healing of our own. But ultimately, the church's primary mission, identity, and ministry is not wrapped up in those of us who are already inside. It is not primarily about our comfort and sense of peace. It is not primarily about our sense of belonging. It is not primarily about doing good deeds or maintaining a cultural heritage. All those priorities, valid as they are, must be a means to serve our primary call: aligning our will with God's, loving as God loves, welcoming as God welcomes.

It is still as simple, breathtaking, life altering, and joy filled as that.

Bread for the Journey
An Online Companion

Think of the resources and sermons available online at www.stephanie
spellers.com/radicalwelcome, as "bread for the journey." These resources
will help you to craft a strategic plan for change, understand the hard work
of inviting, inclusion and radical welcome, and nurture a congregation that
seeks to become a learning, flexible community. You will not travel there
overnight or even in a few weeks or months. But with this treasure trove,
you can better equip yourself and your community to imagine and move
more effectively toward God's dream for you.

Here's what you'll find in the online companion:

- A Welcome Change: The Radical Welcome Workshop
  (6-week version)
- The Power Grid: Tool for Discerning Who Is The Other (exercise)
- Biblical Foundations of Radical Welcome (Bible study)
- Best Practices for Inviting Congregations (list)
- Best Practices for Inclusive Congregations (list)
- Assessment Tool for Studying Your Congregation's Reality and Charting
  Your Dream (questionnaire)
- Meeting Fear with Compassion and Wisdom (exercises)
- Reckoning with Fear and Embracing Change (Bible study)
- The Practices of a Radically Welcoming Community (chart)
- Sermons from Leaders across the Church
- Subject-headed Bibliography

Acknowledgments

There's no way I could have made my own radical welcome journey without the witness, love, and prodding of so very, very many people.

First are the organizations that provided me with funding and support to pursue the Radical Welcome Project: the entire visionary Episcopal crew at Every Voice Network, the first organization to offer me not only funding but a platform for sharing the "radical welcome" vision via a series of web articles in 2003; the Episcopal Evangelical Education Society, including executive director Penny Saffer and my liaison, Michael Morgan, who awarded me an Evangelism for the 21st Century grant and then added an extra boost when I needed it most; Bishops Roy "Bud" Cederholm and Gayle Harris of the Diocese of Massachusetts, who imagined with me and then put their money where their vision was; Episcopal City Mission in the Diocese of Massachusetts, especially Ruy Costa, who provided funding and a broad vision for change. In addition, these groups, along with colleagues and leaders in the Dioceses of Los Angeles and Massachusetts, Episcopal Divinity School, and the Episcopal Church Center in New York, helped me to compile the list of eight congregations I visited as part of the Radical Welcome Project.

By sharing their sermons and talks, these wise and inspiring leaders have enriched me and added to the online companion to this book: Ed Bacon, Tracey Lind, Juan Oliver, Altagracia Perez, Bonnie Perry, Bill Tully, and Crossroads Ministry.

The following people stood with me, cheered for me, prayed for me, questioned me, called me on my own prejudices and privilege, and kept calling to say, "Is it done yet?":

My Church Publishing family, especially Ken Arnold, Susie Erdey and Cynthia Shattuck, and the editors who nurtured this book in its infancy, Joan Castagnone and Johnny Ross;

My Episcopal Divinity School colleagues, especially faculty and staff members Angela Bauer, Steven Charleston, Alcurtis Clark, Nancy Davidge, Ian Douglas, Christopher Duraisingh, Carter Heyward, Sheryl

Kujawa-Holbrook, Elisa Lucozzi, Rick McCall, Kwok Pui Lan, Joan Martin, Ed Rodman, and Fredrica Harris Thompsett; along with classmates and friends like Katrina Browne, Eva Cavaleri, B. K. Hipsher, Elaine McCoy, Lallie Lloyd, Devin McLachlan, Calvin Sanborn, and Greg Wong;

My supporters throughout the Diocese of Massachusetts, including our diocesan visionary, M. Thomas Shaw, bishops Cederholm and Harris, retired bishop and continuing inspiration Barbara Harris, Anoma Abeyaratne, Steven Bonsey (my dear ghost editor), Louise Conant, Michael Dangelo, John and Trish de Beer, Herbert Donovan, Fran Early, Paige Fisher, Pam Foster, Miriam Gelfer, Susan Gershwin, Gregory Jacobs, Brian Murdoch, Julia Slayton, Jep Streit and Dana Whitehead.

Gareth Evans, Titus Presler, Frank Smith, François Trottier, Daniel Velez-Rivera, and the people of St. Peter's Episcopal Church in Cambridge, my first radically welcoming Episcopal home;

The leaders of Trinity Church in the City of Boston; St. Stephen's Episcopal Church in Lynn, Massachusetts; St. Paul's Episcopal Church in Millis, Massachusetts; and the Dioceses of Massachusetts and Pennsylvania and the whole of Province 1 for listening, testing material, reflecting with and teaching me;

Still more friends and loved ones, including Damon Oakley, Rachel Bundang, Jonathan Callard, Mary and Danny Clay, Catherine Clay, Susan Gershwin, Bob Greiner, Kerrie Harthan and Gloria Korsman, Jennifer Hughes, Iza Husin, Julianne Morris, Jennifer Olson, Alison Peacock, J. Ken Stuckey, Daniel Summers, and Victoria Weinstein;

Fran Early, the women of the Greenfire community in Tenants Harbor, Maine, and the brothers of the Society of St. John the Evangelist, based in Cambridge, Burdick's Chocolate in Harvard Square, Starbucks on Boylston in Boston, Papa Razzi in Boston, Earth Matters on Manhattan's Lower East Side, and Café Mona Lisa in Greenwich Village—all of whom provided me with a soul-restoring writers' sanctuary;

The Radical Welcome Project simply would not exist if I hadn't had the blessing to meet and speak with more than 200 Episcopalians and others over a two-year period. Every person revealed some precious nugget of wisdom, another glimpse at the very face of God. These brothers and sisters radically welcomed *me*:

- *At-large:* Paige Blair, Mark Bozzuti-Jones, Sarah Dylan Breuer, Daniel Caballero, Tom Callard, Lisa Cataldo, Eva Cavaleri, Arrington Chambliss, Steven Charleston, Thom Chu, Ruy Costa, Alison Coyle, Michael Dangelo, Ruth Davis, Chitral De Mel, Christopher Duraisingh, Rick Fabian, Norm Faramelli, Douglas Fenton, Pam Foster, Charles Fulton,

Jonathan Galliher, Richard Giles, Allison Grisham Burkepile, Sara Hamlen, Gayle Harris, Andrew Kraemer, Sheryl Kujawa-Holbrook, Eric Law, Sarah Lawton, Jeremy Lucas, Devin McLachlan, Ernesto Medina, Sara Miles, Jane Oasin, Thomas Pang, Bonnie Perry, Michael Poovey, Edward Rodman, Cathy Roskam, Calvin Sanborn, Stefani Schatz-Duggan, Donald Schell, Don Scott, Daniel Simons, Mark Smith, Geoffrey Tristram, SSJE, Bill Tully, Winnie Varghese, Daniel Velez-Rivera, Dana Whiteside, Arthur Williams

- *All Saints Episcopal Church in Pasadena, California:* Stephen Cheney-Rice, Helen Cooper, Joe Duggan, Rusty Harding, Alma Phillips Hill, Christina Honchell, David Jackson, Wilma Jakobsen, Shannon Ferguson Kelly, Zelda Kennedy, Abel Lopez, Justin McNeil, Bob Miller, Milton Molina, Sarah Nichols, George Regas, Susan Russell, Jim White, Monica
- *Church of the Apostles in Seattle, Washington:* Ben Brackin, Lacey Brown, Ryan Marsh, Ray McKechnie, Gwen Owen, Karen Ward, Phil Woodward and others
- *Grace Episcopal Church in Lawrence, Massachusetts:* Elsa Berroa, Sue Boos, Asela Collado, Ennis Duffis, Maria Francisco, Henry Hoffmann, Fran Kuchar, Migdalia Mendez, Frank and Pauline Messer, Leona Sestina, Carol St. Louis
- *Holy Faith Episcopal Church in Inglewood, California:* Kenneth Adams, Patricia Amadi, Alba Luz Bran, Lydia Bran, Rosa Castro, Juan Catarino, Daniel Cole, Wilhemina Cole, Gary Commins, Irene Cowley, Rosalie Danna, Katie de Rose, David Ejimole, Antonia Garcia, Elisa Guevara, Carmen and Mario Henriquez, Bruce Lee, Joanne Leslie, Vilma Manzannres, Daniel Mogbo, Ruth Monette, Elsa Monzon, Robin Mullins, Calvin Nash, Samuel Ojukwu, Gloria Okolangi, Elke Onwudachi, Teresa Penerilas, Guevara Penerilas, Altagracia Perez, Floyd Prince, Melissa Sims, Sybil Stevenson, Denise Williams, Ruby Williams, Brian Yamada
- *St. Bartholomew's Episcopal Church in Atlanta, Georgia:* Matt Bolan, Nancy Baxter, Pat Carol, Pat Curl, Jim Curtis, Beverly Elliott, Charles Gearing, Tim Hendrix, Cal Johnson, Clay and Karen Johnson, Lauren Kretz, Maggie Kulyk, J. R. Lander, Fran Linz, Ken and Kerry Lockerman, Peg Lowman, Bob Maller, Shelley Parnes, Lela May Perry, Tim Peterson, Ruby Phillips, Marilynn Richtarik, Marlon Seward, Jean Smith, Fred and Jane Terry, Arthur Villarreal, Ben Wells, John York
- *St. Mary's Episcopal Church in West Harlem, New York:* Janet Dorman, Barbara Fraser, Charles Kelly, Jenny Knust, Earl and Elizabeth Kooperkamp, Ivory Johnson, Irene McKenzie, Liz Mellen, Bonnie

Phelps, M. Rodriguez, Dorothy Ross, Bill Smith, Gloria Smith, Audrey St. Mark, Jasen and Lillian Townsend, Glenda Marie White

- *St. Paul's Episcopal Church in Duluth, Minnesota:* Laura Amendola, Sue Anderson, Betsy Baumgarten, Beverly and Doug Bennett, Jamie Blodgett, Tony Blodgett, Debbie Bright, Chazz Boykin, Holly and Jason Butcher, Joanne Chesser, Nancy Claypool, Bill and Connie Dinan, Joanne and Ryan Erspamer, Pat Fogel, Lara and Alice Foss, Candace Ginsberg, Jackie Johnson, Elaine Killen, Aron Kramer, Tony Ladeaux, Michelle Lang, Jesse and Naomi Martus, Sarah McGinley, Terry Parsons, Rhoda Robinson, Sue Stromquist, Michelle Sullivan, Toni Thorstad, Andy Topka, Jessica Warpula, Bob Williams
- *St. Philip's Episcopal Church in Harlem, New York:* Chuck Allen, Sidney and Philip Blake-Spivey, Cecily Broderick y Guerra, Courtney Browne, Dorothy Carlton, Willette Carlton, Emily Frye, Tod Roulet, Wendy Sealy, Beatrice Tomlinson

And a special thank you to the people of *St. Paul's Cathedral in Boston, Massachusetts*, The Crossing community at St. Paul's Cathedral, the Diocese of Long Island, General Theological Seminary, the Center for Progressive Renewal, and the Staff of the Presiding Bishop of the Episcopal Church. Thank you all for being my partners and teachers on the radical welcome journey.